Praise for Brooklyn Ran

"A paradigm shift is well underway in how we think about children. And from her deep immersion in young people's lives, Brooklyn Raney offers a rich, detailed, and practical guide for parents, educators, coaches, and youth leaders wanting to build upon this new science of human connection. Her essential message is a beautiful reminder of how powerfully trusted adults affect the lives of young people."

—MICHAEL REICHERT, PhD, psychologist, author of
How to Raise a Boy: The Power of Connection to Raise Good Men

"*One Trusted Adult* is an invaluable resource for educators, parents, and others who want to play a significant and positive role in the lives of young people. Brooklyn Raney combines best practices and the latest research with her experience as the dean of students at an independent school to write *the* resource book for working with youth. It should be required reading for every teacher and school administrator in America."

—CAROLINE HELDMAN, executive director of
The Representation Project, professor at Occidental College

"*One Trusted Adult* should be required reading for anyone who works, will work, might work, is thinking about working, with tweens or teens. Offering solid insight into their development, growth, and needs, it is sprinkled with real-life examples and hands-on tips for dealing with those wonky teenage years. Seasoned with understanding and compassion, it is the Google Maps application for navigating the trusted adult's supportive relationship with his or her charge."

—BETSY BROWN BRAUN, child development and behavior specialist,
author of *Just Tell Me What to Say* and *You're Not the Boss of Me*

"Relationships matter, and for teens growing up in our society today, good relationships with adult models and mentors *really* matter! In *One Trusted Adult*, Brooklyn Raney well uses her keen observations and experiences working in schools and other settings to underscore the critical importance of trusted adult mentors and models in the lives of adolescents. The importance of this topic, and book, can't be overstated."

—THOMAS G. PLANTE, PhD, ABPP, Augustin Cardinal Bea,
S.J. University Professor and professor of psychology, Santa Clara University
and adjunct clinical professor of psychiatry, Stanford University

"Here is the guide to having meaningful conversations with young people that we have always wanted and sorely needed. Raney delivers important advice on navigating relationships within diverse groups of people and in a range of settings and circumstances. Her approach will leave you educated and empowered."
—DR. MAURA CULLEN, diversity and inclusion specialist, author of *35 Dumb Things Well-Intended People Say*

"It is critical that adults everywhere are committed to being trusted allies to the young people they work with, care about, and love but it's even more essential to learn how to do so in a healthy, ethical, and empathy-filled way. Raney breaks down what is potentially one of the trickiest relationships to develop and maintain in a brave, thoughtful, and stirring read. *One Trusted Adult* will have you laughing, crying, and ultimately better prepared to make a difference in the lives of young people you care about. What a gift!"
—GRACE GLOR, domestic and sexual violence prevention educator

"Young people have incredibly high expectations for the adults they allow into their lives. There is no question the impact that a trusted adult has on our youth today and Brooklyn describes this perfectly in *One Trusted Adult*. Brooklyn homes in on the mindsets, changes, and perceptions that our youth have, how they navigate through their daily life, and what those relationships truly mean to them. This is a must-read for educators, parents, coaches, counselors, and anyone who has working relationships with children!"
—BRITTNEY MANGIERI, associate director of counseling, EF Academy

"In *One Trusted Adult*, Brooklyn Raney provides an inspiring road map to help caring adults navigate their journeys in working with young people. She offers timely cues and clues to cultivate and nourish trust in young people by skillfully weaving narrative and research with practical time-tested strategies. Brooklyn walks the talk, informing readers of best practices as she echoes the importance of adult self-reflection and a generous understanding of young people to create lasting connections. *One Trusted Adult* is a must-read that resonates loud and clear in an age where it is essential for caring adults to foster and facilitate growth in young people."
—JOHN YEAGER, CEO, The Yeager Leadership Group, coauthor of *SMART Strengths: Building Character, Resilience and Relationships in Youth*

One Trusted Adult

One Trusted Adult

How to Build Strong Connections
· AND ·
Healthy Boundaries with Young People

Brooklyn Raney

For information on bulk orders of this book, go to www.brooklynraney.com

Some names and identifying details have been changed to protect the privacy of individuals. Although the author and publisher have made every effort to ensure that the information in this book was correct at press time, the author and publisher do not assume and hereby disclaim any liability to any party for any loss, damage, or disruption caused by errors or omissions, whether such errors or omissions result from negligence, accident, or any other cause. This book is not intended as a substitute for the medical advice of physicians or the legal advice of attorneys.

Library of Congress Control Number:2019913844

Printed in the United States of America

ISBN 978-1-7332025-1-0

Cover design by Mark Reis

Text design by Jamie McKee

*For my parents and the many trusted adults
who played an important role in my story.
And for the young people who have chosen to trust me.*

Contents

Foreword

If you have opened the pages of *One Trusted Adult*, you care. You care about having healthy relationships with young people. You care about young people's well-being and believe they deserve to have at least one adult who can support them as they navigate the complexities of growing up.

We desperately need more adults in education and youth services who not only have the passion and dedication to do right by young people but the skills to make it a reality. Because it's not enough to have the desire to be that one trusted adult. The work is hard and it is complicated. Sometimes it can feel like it's not worth doing or that the institutions you are working in lack the skill or intention to prioritize young people's welfare. You can feel alone, confused, or worried.

This doesn't mean the work isn't worth doing. I have spent my career dedicated to teaching and learning from young people and never regretted it. We all just need a constant source of common-sense wisdom and applicable skills to help us do our best work and, in turn, help the young people who depend on us. Those skills and wisdom are what you will find here. Brooklyn Raney wrote *One Trusted Adult* for you. She has spent years in schools navigating similar terrain. She has been a teacher, coach, camp counselor, and administrator and is now sharing with you all she has learned from those experiences.

As you will read in these pages, being a trusted adult requires striving to understand the world of young people and how to best manage ourselves within it. Think about how challenging and complex our responsibilities are. We need to know when to offer a young person more hands-on support and when to let them fall—hopefully, with an appropriate net underneath them. We need to maintain good boundaries with young people, especially if they haven't had other adults they can rely on. When they make big mistakes we have to hold them accountable while showing them a way to make amends and believe in a future they can feel positive about.

It's also true that, in spite of investing our hearts into these people, they will do things that make us so angry and disappointed we will struggle to not take their behavior personally. I will never forget my first teaching experiences when a young person I adored lied to me, or was mean to another student, or didn't complete a task I really needed them to do. It was hard to remember that their actions were not a reflection of me or my teaching ability. After all, I would think to myself, they knew what my values were and what I expected of them, how could they disappoint me like this? I look back on those moments and laugh . . . at myself. Their behavior wasn't about me. It was about where they were in that moment of time; they needed me to be the adult who could see the larger picture and hold them accountable in a way that would mean something to them, without my ego or my own emotional baggage getting in the way.

One Trusted Adult will challenge you and your approach to your work. It can be so hard for educators to admit what we don't know, what we are confused about, or when we make mistakes. Somehow, we are supposed to know everything it takes to be a great educator. Somehow, we are never supposed to mess up because "it's all about the kids." And the fear of making a mistake is real, from disappointing ourselves to interacting with angry parents to worrying about our job security.

You need information so you can see the problems on the horizon, hopefully before they walk through your door or you receive an email about a student that makes you sigh and put your head on the table. It's inevitable that we will be blindsided by problems with the children in our charge. We all go through this and we all need support.

This book also compels us to look at the institutions in which we work. We can't ignore the reality that some adults in our schools and youth-serving institutions abuse young people. We can't shy away from this reality, as much as it frightens or disgusts us. As educators who want to keep young people safe, we have to know how to ask ourselves really uncomfortable questions like: What happens if we get a bad feeling in our stomach about a colleague? How and when should we report what we know to our supervisors? What do we need to know about child safety and what can we do to take a commonsense approach to this problem without thinking the worst of everyone?

Less frightening but so problematic is that we have to acknowledge that young people often interact with other adults who are not the role models they should, and sometimes claim, to be. Of course, young people see some adults misbehaving on the national level, via news stories or popular media, but we have to admit that young people experience this same problem with adults in their own communities. For better or worse, they are watching us. When I ask young people in my classes and presentations if they have seen an adult in a position of authority dominate, humiliate, or undermine children, almost all of them, wherever I go, raise their hands. Ironically, they also report that these same adults are the ones who talk most about respect. As if a child will actually respect an adult because they are forced to show respect. And young people see other adults who don't stand up to the troubling behavior of their colleagues—even though we tell young people if they see bullying of any kind they should tell an adult.

All of this is the reality of working with young people. It always has been.

You may be reading this and wondering why you are in this profession or thinking that what you're about to read is going to be really heavy lifting. Far from it. You will read ways to feel less anxious and more empowered to have the relationships you want to have with the young people in your life. You will be better equipped to handle those really difficult moments with other adults in your institutions. I don't think there's truly a choice about this. We have to be the adults our young people deserve.

—Rosalind Wiseman

Introduction

Young people are like disco balls. They slowly spin and reflect what surrounds them. They assemble all the little pieces of what they see, eventually forming a larger picture, a personal perspective and identity all their own. Infants have only a few people in their lives and not much choice in what they reflect, but adolescents see their world expand, and they begin to choose who and what surrounds them; they begin to decide what they reflect and who they will become.

Although parents work hard for their piece of mirror, during adolescence—a time of growth and natural liberation—young people begin to resist parental influence. We know that this resistance is a normal part of growth and development, and eventually young people come back around and fully value their parents' thoughts, opinions, and experiences. In adolescence, however, extra pieces on that identity-forming disco ball reflect the things and the people the young person chooses to surround themselves with. That might be social media feeds, video games, celebrities, friends and classmates, or, if we are lucky, a trusted adult.

If you're reading this book, you have already taken the first step toward the role of trusted adult in a young person's life. You are showing interest in how to do it well—and that is what we are going to tackle: best practices for being a trusted adult in the life of a young person. The harder we work to build the trust of adolescents, the larger the piece of the mirror we get reflecting the values and approach to life we hope to teach. I'm here to tell you that working with young people isn't easy, and the capacity to do it well isn't innate. I believe in training. I believe in practice. I believe in partnership.

As a dean of students at an independent school for the better part of the last decade, I went to work every day thinking I had seen it all—and then something more outrageous would happen. Several times throughout my time as a dean I had the same conversation:

Teacher: "Another late night in the office, Brook?"

Me: "Oh yeah, just when I thought I had seen it all ..."

Teacher: "Well, if nothing else, it will make a great chapter in your book someday!"

The student situations I encountered ranged from the silliest to the scariest: from adolescent choices that made you just shake your head and smile, to those that made your stomach flip and your heart stop. I share many of these stories throughout the book to illustrate the world that adolescents face today—stories about hook-up culture, social media, substance abuse, and threats of suicide. The path each adolescent will walk and the risks they will face will look different, but no matter the risk and no matter the path, the research tells us the presence of a trusted adult in a young person's life has significant value.

I never set out to turn these stories and my experience into a book. I am an educator. I am in the trenches of this work with you. Evidence of this is in the number of places this book was written. Physically, it has been written outside drum practice, in ski lodges, at public libraries, in theaters during auditions, in school parking lots, between meetings, late at night, and in dentists' offices. If you are a parent or anyone who works with youth, you will understand this. Really, though, this book has been written over the last ten years of gathering the stories of students, campers, athletes, and adolescents I have encountered in my work. I am a mother, aunt, educator, coach, volunteer, mentor (formally and informally), and a trusted adult to many young people. Through my experiences in these roles—the successes and the failures—I have come to strongly believe that the presence of a well-trained, boundaried, and reliable trusted adult in the life of each and every young person will change this world for the better, and so I have set out to prove it.

I have written this book for my eighteen-year-old self as a first-time local day camp counselor, for my twenty-two-year-old self as a first-time live-in nanny, for my twenty-four-year-old self as a terrified first-time educator at a boarding school, for my twenty-five-year-old self as a first-time hockey coach (who thought she knew it all), for my twenty-eight-year-old self as a newly appointed and underexperienced dean of students, for my current self as a parent, camp director, speaker and consultant, and, most importantly, for the educator, parent, and trusted adult I aspire to be. I have needed a book like this, packed with practical advice, real-life scenarios, and deep context, to guide me in my work with young people through all my ages and in all my roles.

The time, energy, and work I have invested in the growth of the young people in my care has always led to an equal amount of much-needed growth in me. Young people bring out the best in me, even through the challenges, questioning, and disappointment. When I refer to young people in this book, I am talking about all the tweens, teens, and young adults you may have relationships with—students, advisees, campers, players, nieces, nephews, children, grandchildren, neighbors, and friends. Although many of the stories come from boarding school, summer camp, and parenting, I hope they resonate with you and reveal how to step in, show up, and be there for young people in all areas of your connections with youth. We all have room to improve and make the most of our moments with youth, and as the world shifts and changes, so must we.

Looking back, I recognize that I hit the jackpot when it comes to trusted adults. In every phase of my youth, I can identify multiple adults in my life who served in both formal and informal roles—and I could turn to these people about anything. From my own parents to coaches, teachers, school secretaries, camp counselors, lifeguards, babysitters, aunts, uncles, grandparents, friends' parents, and neighbors, I had no shortage of good, wholesome, grown-up humans who made me feel seen, heard, and valued. Through my work as a consultant for schools and camps, I have learned that my situation is rare. Many people I meet cannot identify a single adult from their middle school or high school years who they say they trusted wholeheartedly.

If you grew up without a trusted adult in your life, are you destined to fail? Absolutely not. But having such an adult in your life when you are young can significantly reduce risk, give you a safe place for processing normal life questions, provide a teacher and model of important life skills, and help you calibrate your inner compass. All of the benefits of having a trusted adult are proven to assist young people in growing up to be individuals who can manage emotion, develop healthy relationships, and contribute positively to their communities. Being there for young people, just being there, is a small ask that yields an enormous gain. This commitment, the commitment of being there in a trusted and responsible way for the young people in your world, is not a new concept, but if we all truly train for it and commit to it, we can make big, positive changes in a world facing too many school shootings, overdoses, and suicides.

Unfortunately, some adults in positions of power have used their status to take advantage of children, and we have seen these abuses exposed in news headlines. Jerry Sandusky and Larry Nassar are among the individuals who have sexually and emotionally abused the young people in their care, and fortunately will serve prison time for their crimes. The Boy Scouts, the Catholic Church, and independent boarding schools are organizations that have been called out for their silence, and for allowing abuse to occur within their institutions. These are the same organizations that have sworn to protect children, and whose missions claim to build up and empower youth. I have sat with the victims of abuse in these schools and organizations, I have listened to their stories, and I have witnessed their pain.

As a parent, I find that stories like this make me pause. Should I really be handing over my son into the care of other adults? Does the benefit outweigh the risk? Any time I stop to ask myself these questions, I meet another trusted adult who reminds me exactly what this role should entail and precisely what a grounded, positive, boundaried, well-trained adult looks like. Meeting incredible teachers, coaches, camp counselors, ministers, music instructors, and more reminds me why I should work to surround my son with as many trusted adults as possible. His connection to adults outside the family will only strengthen the relationships inside our family. As difficult as it is to imagine that I may not always be what my son needs, I must accept that his turning to adults he trusts is a sign of his growing independence and curiosity, and proof that he is moving along his own path toward adulthood.

· · · · ·

Finally, I think it is important that you know how I identify, so you can recognize the path I have walked to get to this place and the lens through which I view the world. I am a cisgender, heterosexual, white woman in my mid-thirties living in New Hampshire after growing up in Canada. I am married to a man, and I have one adopted son, who you will hear plenty about in this book. It is important to me that you know he has given me full permission to use the stories about him that I share. He told me, "If it might help someone else, then go for it." This statement made me proud, but I am still waiting for him to ask me for a snowboard in return for his permission (at least I hope it's a snowboard and not a snowmobile—he *is* an unpredictable adolescent after all).

Throughout the book I will often use the word "they" as a singular pronoun. Sometimes I do this because that is the way an individual has asked to be represented, sometimes to protect the gender of the person in the story I am sharing, and mostly to not assume or place anyone in the gender binary without knowing for certain how they identify.

Though this book was written with the intention of readers moving through the chapters from beginning to end, it can also be used as a reference, with chosen sections read as needed. The early chapters describe what we are up against with the growing brains and growing pains of adolescents, and provides strategies we can use to work our way into the sphere of young people by building trust and opening up conversations.

The second section uncovers ways in which some adults have exploited their responsibility as trusted adults and teaches you how to build boundaries, report inappropriate behavior, and model being a trusted, reliable adult for young people.

In the final section, we explore the importance of pursuing partnerships with people outside the organization or school, how to cultivate important life skills conversations, the necessity of building teams of trusted adults open to giving and receiving feedback, and how to evaluate and celebrate the people and things you want to encourage. Whether you read this book in one sitting or turn to it over a span of years, I want you to hear loud and clear that building trust and establishing boundaries is a simultaneous process. The thoughtful and intentional layering of trust and boundaries is what young people most need from you.

By providing tips, tricks, tactics, and strategies for building trust, establishing boundaries, and creating a positive culture with young people, *One Trusted Adult* helps you understand adolescents better, question yourself less, act confidently in your interactions and communication, and be grateful for the privilege of the incredible work you get to do with young people. Thank you for joining me on this journey, for being a champion for youth, for committing to support the next generation, and for promising to just be there for the young people in your life.

Part I
Building Trust

CHAPTER 1

Predictably Unpredictable

It was 2 p.m. on a Tuesday afternoon when I got a call from the nurse to come pick up my sixth-grade son from school.

"Is he sick?"

"We can discuss his well-being when you get here," the nurse said, leaving no opportunity for further questioning.

As an educator, I knew this was code for "something's up."

When I arrived at the school I was taken into a room, and the nurse began asking me questions about my parenting.

"Do you get angry with your son in a way that you don't get angry with others? Do you or your husband call him names? Would you rate your punishments and consequences at home as harsh?"

"I don't think so," I replied, suddenly feeling as though I was being accused of neglecting or abusing my son.

"Your son has made a mistake that violates school rules, and at this time he is very scared and nervous to tell you. He even shared that you can be *unpredictable* at times."

"Okay. Well, whatever it is, I am sure we can work through it." I fully understood the nurse's concerns at this point, and I was also very familiar with the brilliant tactics my eleven-year-old could deploy to avoid facing the consequences of his choices. (I would love to tell you about his infraction, however, this is the one event he has asked me not to share. Someday, when he's older and can find humor in his school violation, maybe he and I will cowrite a second edition that includes his sixth-grade shenanigans! For now, you will have to trust that his minor infraction was a perfect example of an underdeveloped frontal lobe doing its finest work.)

The nurse was able to mediate a conversation between me and my son where he shared his recent actions and the spiral of events they caused. We reached an agreement on school and home consequences that everyone felt was fair. When we got in the car, of course, I had one important question for him:

"Did you share with the nurse that I can be unpredictable?"

"Yes."

"I am curious to know what that means to you. I think, from what you shared, the nurse thinks I am unpredictably neglectful and abusive."

"You are."

"How so?"

"Well . . . I mean . . . you're just unpredictable. If I break the rules, I have no idea if you aren't going to let me play video games, or if you're going to take my iPod away, or if I'm not going to get to go to a friend's house this weekend. Wouldn't you call that *unpredictable?*"

Oh, the joys of parenting, educating, coaching, and advising young people! It's hazardous work without any of the hazard pay. Life with adolescents is an epic dance party, scary roller coaster, military battlefield, and the warmest hug ever, all mixed into one. And for each young person, every day, hour, and minute can be cataloged as one of those activities—or something we have never even seen before. In our work to build trust with young people we must match their unpredictability with a thoughtful approach that is both individualized and flexible, if we are going to maximize our impact. Solidifying what we know, admitting what we don't know, and asking young people what they think we should know are three practical ways to combat the youthful unpredictability we fear without squashing the blissful and creative youthful unpredictability we love.

We Don't Know What We Don't Know

When I was six years old, and my brother and I were anxiously awaiting the arrival of our next sibling, we decided what would be best was actually a dog. We let our mother know our preference; instead of a new little sibling, we would rather that she deliver a dog. She was due in December, and this would serve as our Christmas present as well. It was a win-win.

All the adults we encountered thought this was cute, and did not correct us or adjust our understanding of human pregnancy and the circle of life. We continued to imagine our mother as a vending machine that could produce what we'd decided. On December 4, 1991, when our grandparents took us to the hospital to meet our new puppy, we could not contain our excitement. We ran into our mom's hospital room, snow boots clunking, and our mother introduced us to our baby sister, Brianne. We immediately started booing. That's right, in unison, with thumbs pointed down, a chorus of two chanted, "Booooooooooooooooo." Welcome to the world, Brianne! Rough start. She maintains the nickname BooBoo to this day. We did not know what we did not know, and poor BooBoo knew even less.

Young people get a bad rap for believing they know it all. They wholeheartedly believe they have the world figured out. They believe they know what is best. They believe they are invincible. Didn't you? I like to describe stages of growth using the human relationship with questions. At some point in our middle school experience—after years of pummeling our parents with questions, beginning when we were toddlers—we stop asking all the questions and, instead, start answering. We answer questions confidently, whether we are right or wrong. Somewhere in our twenties, when our brains develop further, we leave the safety of the daily school schedule and the luxury of living on our parents' paychecks, and we are swiftly knocked to the ground by reality. We are back to a place of asking more questions than answering, and back to a place of feeling like we have zero understanding of the world.

Before you dive fully into this book, reflect on your adolescent self—remember the joy and arrogance of knowing it all. Imagine the educators and adults who had the privilege and pain of working with you. The bright eyes of these adolescents bursting with confidence in their own knowledge should fuel us as adults rather than annoy us. Though it's true that, when you, as the adult, have already had a certain experience and you feel you have the answers to adolescents' life questions, it can be frustrating not to be able to gift that knowledge to a young person. But they are resistant to receiving the full bounty of your wisdom for a reason.

When baby birds are born, they have a small "egg tooth" on their beak. Their survival depends on them breaking out of their shell using this extra tooth. If a parent bird were to break the shell and help the baby bird, it would likely die. That would not be so helpful. The stress, work, and skills the little birds build as they break out of their shells are part of the process that helps them survive. It strengthens them. And they already have all the tools they need to complete the task. When the bird finally breaks all the way through, the egg tooth falls off the beak; this tool is no longer needed.

When advising young people through events we have already faced ourselves, we must remind ourselves that they are writing their own stories, charting their own journeys, and building a set of tools and skills they will need in adulthood. They don't just lose their innocence, they whittle it away, experience by experience. They don't decide to switch back from question answerer to question asker; this event comes with a tumble after a run-in with reality. Stepping aside and recognizing that all humans only know what they know until they figure things out for themselves relieves us of the pressure of teaching everything, reminds us of the need to build safe spaces for exploration, and allows us to enjoy stories like the following:

I was sitting at the kitchen table with two friends and their four-year-old nephew. Suddenly, my friend's computer died and he lost a document he had been working on all day. Abruptly, he shouted, "Sh*t! I *hate* this computer!"

Stopped dead in his cereal-eating tracks, the four-year-old looked up and shouted, "You said HATE!"

Hate was a naughty word in this boy's family. His parents had trained him not to use it. They had trained him so well, in fact, that he was completely unaware of his uncle's cussing.

We don't know what we don't know, until we come to know it. When we were young, we were given the chance to carve our own individual and unique path, and so, too, should our students. We must give them the chance to come to know what they need to know, day by day, and moment by moment, sharpening their beaks along the way.

We Still Don't Know What We Don't Know

If we adults think adolescents know little, and they think they know it all, what do they think of what we know? If you are a parent, you are aware that most young people think adults know nothing and are completely oblivious to the "real world." At times, generational differences in clothing, language, and music make it feel as though there is no one "real world" but instead multiple worlds in which people live parallel existences. Living beside each other, not fully understanding each other, we need to "code-switch" in order to enter another generation's world. One coded language is spoken to grandparents, while another coded language is spoken to peers. Advancing technology seems to be growing the size of this gap exponentially. The things young people once went to adults to ask about, they can now find answers to on their phones. The reasons young people need to reach out to adults have lessened, and the speed of pop culture trends keeps adults always a step (or three) behind.

I have intense memories of the frustrating feeling that the adults in my life were three steps behind. In my strongest memory, I was fifteen and at a campus activities fair, which was being held in a giant field. All the clubs from school were there, advertising their missions and causes in order to recruit new members. A teacher of mine walked toward me with an older gentleman who had been a guest speaker in our class that day. She asked me to explain to him what the activities fair was all about. The man had a hearing aid, and with the music blaring, his only hope of hearing me was to look to the ground and turn his ear toward my mouth. During one of these moments when I was speaking, a Frisbee flew across the field and hit me square in the face. He didn't notice. Neither did my teacher. As my eyes welled up and my lip swelled at rapid speed, I just kept talking. Another student ran over, grabbed the Frisbee, threw out half an apology, and continued on.

I remember keeping up the conversation but thinking in my head, "Does he not know I just got smashed in the face with a Frisbee? Can he not see me crying? Does my teacher not see the size of my lip right now?" This is how I felt about the adults surrounding me in middle and high school. "Do you not see what is happening right under your noses?!" I remember overwhelming frustration, believing that the adults in my life knew nothing but should know everything. When I walked into class the next day and that same teacher from the field said, "Brook, what happened to your face?," I lost all faith in adults. But why didn't I share with them in the moment that I had been hit in the face with the Frisbee? Why did I expect them to know, though I was not willing to share?

Young people have incredibly high expectations for the adults they allow into their lives. Now that I am on the other side of the grown-up fence, I understand that there is a lot we know and plenty we don't. I am sure that, in my time as an educator, I have missed plenty of Frisbees. When we have our eye on dozens, or even hundreds, of students, it is impossible to know it all. We set our relationships with young people up for the greatest potential success by admitting this from the beginning. With struggling adolescents, the symptoms are not always clearly linked to the cause. Providing opportunities for connection, sharing your story, admitting your limitations, and letting your young people know that it is impossible for you to be everywhere, see everything, and know everything about their lives means that you are less likely to not break any promises or let anyone down. As a trusted adult, you are only as useful as the information young people are willing to give you.

A great opening line in your work with young people is, "You know what you know from your experiences, and I know what I know from my experiences. Let's meet in the middle and see if we can learn something from each other."

So yes, I am letting you off the hook here, early in this book. You are not a superhero. You do not have magical powers. You cannot be everything to everyone. Admitting this to yourself and to others on the front end will free you up to face the unpredictability of young people with realistic expectations, flexibility, and a common understanding that neither of you knows it all.

Ask Them!

When you are in doubt about what young people need or how they are feeling, ask them. We ask kids what they want to eat, what classes they want to take, and what position they want to play, but rarely do we ask them how we can best meet their needs as a trusted adult in their lives. Remember—adolescents are rightfully unsettled. Their interests, likes and dislikes, and desires shift constantly, so even when we think we know, or we knew yesterday, we don't know today.

Have you ever had a conversation that goes like this?

"I grabbed you a turkey sandwich so you can eat on the road and we can get to ski lessons on time."

"I don't like turkey."

"But last week when I got you a turkey sandwich, you liked it."

"Well . . . I don't like turkey now."

It is not our fault for not knowing; such changes are a natural part of young people growing into who they are. They try an identity on and take it off again almost as often as they change clothes.

I run a Girls' Leadership Camp, and at the end of camp each summer, we invite parents to a special talk. Camp staff has spent the week with the girls power posing, building picnic tables with power tools, climbing mountains, tackling tough conversations, and pumping these young people up with all the self-confidence and self-esteem they need to last them until we see them again. Before we put these wild wonders back in the hands of their parents, we want to make sure their parents are equipped to embrace and build upon this good work. When my friend and colleague Shanterra McBride stands up before the parents and walks through youth needs, releasing parents from the burden of protecting and saving their child, there is always at least one dad who cries. We are on an eight-year streak! The moment they typically shed tears is when Shanterra says this:

When your child comes home from school crying, and you want to put on your armor and ride out of your castle on a horse to take down anyone who has hurt her, I need you to resist that temptation and simply do this: Ask her, Is there something you need me to do, or do you just want me to listen?

In this moment, you can feel a release of air, energy, and grip. Suddenly, these parents have been given permission to ask their child what they need, instead of feeling that they should know innately what the child needs. Trusted adults who are not the parents of the young people crying in their office can and should operate in exactly the same way: "Is there something you need me to do? Or do you just want me to listen?" Put these words on repeat in your head—they will serve you well.

One day last fall, a new head of school from an all-boys boarding school on the West Coast called me for some advice. He had learned that a year earlier, a young man had died by suicide on their campus. During the call he asked great questions: How do we memorialize the young man without promoting the idea of suicide? How can we meet the needs of the boys who knew him, and the boys who didn't? How do we handle the one-year anniversary? These are all tough questions, and, unfortunately, many schools have had to face them following tragedy. My first question to him was, "Have you asked your students what they need?"

He paused for a long time. He hadn't. He felt an enormous burden to do this work for them. From the outside, it was easy for me to see that part of the boys' grieving process would be working through these questions with their new head of school, instead of him doing it all for them. Remember the baby bird beak? This was the hard work that was going to strengthen the social and emotional development of these boys, and no one could or should do it for them. In consultation with a grief counselor and trauma specialist, the school formed a small committee of boys who were exactly the ones who needed and wanted to do this work. They felt ownership, responsibility, and leadership, all while the head of school was able to serve in a supporting role, knowing that the needs of the students were being met because they had a place to voice them.

Asking these questions in the right way can be key to receiving honest answers that you can translate into action. Looking to improve our camp programming, I used to ask young people: "What is it like to be a middle schooler today?" What a terrible question. I never got answers I could do anything with. They don't know what it's like to be a middle schooler today because they don't really know what it's like to be anything else. Instead, when I ask, "What's awesome about being twelve?" Or "What's the worst about being twelve?" I get juicy answers, full of stories that help paint a picture of this young person's life and the areas where they might need support. It's okay not to have the answers, but it's not okay to not ask the questions.

What Do They Need?

Although we, as adults in the lives of young people, recognize that an individual approach is best for each young person in each moment, we also know that there are universal youth needs that, regardless of generational gaps, technology, and growing and changing young people, remain the foundation of healthy, happy youth.

The most comprehensive list of universal youth needs I have found was developed by the Center for Youth Development and Research in collaboration with the Youth Development Institute. By providing a roof over a child's head and food on the table, adults sometimes let themselves off the hook—they check off that "needs met" box in their heads, assuming that by supplying essential human physiological requirements, plus some love, they are doing a great job. The list of Universal Youth Needs, however, provides a fuller picture—and gives us specifics—of what else we, as adults, can do to ensure that kids are growing into their potential.

UNIVERSAL YOUTH NEEDS

1. **Safety and Structure** A perception that one is safe in the world and that daily events are somewhat predictable
2. **Belonging and Membership** A perception that one values and is valued by others in the family and in the community
3. **Self-Worth and Ability to Contribute** A perception that one is a "good person" who contributes to self and others
4. **Self-Awareness and Spirituality** A perception that one is unique and is intimately attached to extended families, cultural groups, communities, higher deities, and/or principles
5. **Independence and Control Over One's Life** A perception that one has control over daily events and is accountable for one's own actions and for the consequences one's actions have on others
6. **A Close Lasting Relationship with at Least One Adult** A perception that one has a strong and stable relationship with an adult
7. **Competence and Mastery** A perception that one is building skills and that one is "making it" and will succeed in the future

In an interview about Universal Youth Needs, Shanterra McBride, my camp colleague and founder of Marvelous University, which offers life coaching and success planning for young people, stated, "Notice that this list is not called the 'universal youth needs for *positive* youth development.' When it comes to the basic physical and social needs of young people, we should remember, they will get their needs met with or without us, in *positive* or *negative* ways."

McBride continued, sharing the following example:

One of the basic youth needs is Belonging and Membership, which means youth need to know they are cared about by others and feel a sense of connection to others in the group. This means the way young people get this need met could be by wearing the T-shirt of a club they're in at school. It could also mean wearing the colors of the local street gang they're a member of. The school club and street gang are meeting the same need, *they are cared about by others and feel a sense of connection to others in the group.* We may not agree with how their need is getting met, but we have to remember young people will get their needs met with or without us.

Knowing this should inspire us, as adults in the lives of young people, to enter into conversations, show up, understand the full list of universal youth needs, and actively create opportunities for young people to fulfill these needs in positive and healthy ways.

Throughout this book, we will identify the factors that challenge and interfere with our ability to meet the spectrum of youth needs. While keeping at the forefront of our thinking young people's unpredictability and the necessity of individualizing our work with youth, we will identify the tools and tactics that help adults meet young people where they are and give them the guidance they need to flourish.

CHAPTER 2

Growing Brains, Growing Pains

On one particularly memorable day as a dean, I had trouble convincing myself that the students were seeking to meet their own needs, and instead I just thought all hell had broken loose. The day began with a call from a local police officer who was with one of our students. The student, who was not supposed to have his keys, was in the ditch with an upside-down car. Everyone was okay, but it was a scary situation. He risked hurting himself and the consequences of breaking the rules on a bad weather day, all for a McDonald's breakfast sandwich he had been craving.

From the side of the road, I was called to the health center because another student, attempting to jump a fence instead of taking the time to walk around, had cut open her head on the sidewalk. After that, I was called into a classroom because a student had said something horribly offensive to another student in order to make his buddies laugh. Although he recognized his mistake and apologized, much emotional repair work needed to be done. From the classroom, I was called to the dorm because a student, who I had already been working with on this particular theft situation, had "taken matters into her own hands and stolen back what was rightfully hers," causing massive relational disruption and a dorm divided.

While in the dorm I got called back to the health center because a student who was subject to random urinalysis due to a string of substance violations was caught bringing in a bottle of someone else's clean urine in place of her own. From there, I was called to the police station because it was reported that one of my students was operating an illegal business—buying "toys of a sexual nature" in bulk online and selling to locals. Would you believe in my career the words, "I support your entrepreneurial spirit, and would love to assist you in gaining the legal approval to start a business, as long as we can agree on something more appropriate to sell than sex toys" actually came out of my mouth?

The day continued like this, moving from one crisis to the next as I tried to untangle the motives behind the decisions of these growing brains, and working toward resolution and learning. On this day, it was impossible to simply see adolescents attempting to get their needs met, especially because they were working on meeting them in all of the most painful ways. Looking back, however, I can see clearly where these students were seeking to serve their needs of belonging and membership, self-worth, competence, and independence. This fact does not change the consequences, but it has certainly changed my understanding of their choices.

Multiple factors disrupt and confuse young people trying to meet their own needs, and these factors test their courage, education, maturity, and character. Adolescents are bombarded (as we all are) by confusing societal messages about who they are supposed to be and how they are supposed to behave as they navigate a complex and sometimes dangerous world. But unlike most adults, young people are navigating with a set of tools that isn't yet fully sharpened—their brains are still growing.

Dating back as far as Aristotle and Shakespeare and continuing to current researchers and professors, the teenage brain has remained a fascinating area of study. The subject even made its way onto the cover of *National Geographic* in October 2011, when the magazine reported that a study performed by the National Institutes of Health showed that our "brains undergo a massive reorganization between our 12th and 25th years." The article shared that the brain actually does not physically grow much after the age of six, but "as we move through adolescence, the brain undergoes extensive remodeling, resembling a network and wiring upgrade." According to the reporting, "when this development proceeds normally, we get better at balancing impulse, desire, goals, self-interest, rules, ethics, and even altruism, generating behavior that is more complex and, sometimes at least, more sensible. But at times, and especially at first, the brain does this work clumsily. It's hard to get all those new cogs to mesh."

Laurence Steinberg, one of the world's leading experts on adolescence and a professor of psychology at Temple University, notes in his book *Age of Opportunity: Lessons from the New Science of Adolescence* that during early childhood the brain is being built rapidly as vision, language, and gross motor skills improve, and in adolescence the brain is learning to handle a different, though equally important, set of tasks. He urges adults to understand the importance of our work with these growing brains: "We now know that adolescence is a similarly remarkable period of brain reorganization and plasticity. This discovery is enormously important, with far-reaching implications for how we parent, educate, and treat young people. If the brain is especially sensitive to experience during adolescence, we must be exceptionally thoughtful and careful about the experiences we give people as they develop from childhood into adulthood."

The behaviors we see in young people are often a product of this growing, clumsy brain. It is normal to witness adolescents make new choices, take different actions and speak different words from what we expected of the child, and try on new identities as their brains form and solidify a relationship with risks and rewards. Understanding the science behind the choices of young people helps us to navigate our work with them, but it does not make it any less frustrating when we see a young person make decisions we know will serve them poorly.

As I travel from school to school, outlining the concept and practice of One Trusted Adult in professional development sessions with faculty teams, I love to facilitate an activity I call the Youth Risk Battle, in which educators debate their chief concerns about the complex challenges these growing brains are navigating.

The Youth Risk Battle

In a group of adults, ask individuals to write down three things they believe to be the biggest risks facing young people today. They can choose from the list below, or they can provide their own concerns. The big question they are answering is: What do you worry most will get in the way of the young people you work with achieving their definition of success? When they are finished, ask the individuals to pair with another group member and combine their two lists of three concerns into one list of three. When that is complete, ask the group to come together as a whole (ten at most) and battle it out to create one list of three risks.

Through this exercise, you will get at the root of concerns that adults share for the young people they work with in your organization. Because they must battle to keep their risk on the list, you will learn deeper reasons for why your team holds these particular worries for the specific youth you serve.

A twist on this exercise is facilitating it with teens and adults. Ask the key question to young people this way: "What do you worry most about getting in the way of the success of your peers?" The conversation between adult and young person can result in fascinating discoveries for both parties. The long list below captures the plethora of issues that dominate news stories and schools today:

peer pressure	harassment	nicotine use
risk-seeking	hyper-sexualization	alcohol use
behavior	objectification	illegal drug use
hormonal confusion	negative body	obesity
overscheduling	image	physical abuse
technology	suicide	poverty
addiction	low self-esteem	apathy
physical health	porn culture	lack of resources
emotional health	substance abuse	vaping
bullying	college pressure	unhealthy home life
concussions	illegal behavior	access to weapons
insufficient sleep	cars and risky	school shootings
stress	driving	sexual identity
lack of nutrition	mental health	abusive
cyberbullying	sexual assault	relationships
hazing	pregnancy	

It seems a little ridiculous, doesn't it? Debating which risks are the riskiest? But what happens in the session is an incredible sharing of experience, concern, worry, fear, and deep knowledge and understanding of the adolescent world, colleague to colleague. No matter where I travel, the short list almost always includes these three concerns:

1. Technology and social media
2. Porn and hook-up culture
3. Mental health and anxiety

Below, I want to dive deeper into each of these concerns and unpack what is happening in the adolescent world. If we can better understand the problems, and the growing pains that come along with these growing brains, we will be better equipped to find and build solutions.

Technology and Social Media

What I find fascinating about the conversation surrounding technology and young people is that we blame young people for the problems: "He's always on his phone," "We can't pull him away from the video games," "She was not being very nice to people online." Adults created the technology, adults bought the technology, and adults gave the technology to the kids in their care. Then adults became angry, upset, and worried about the ways young people are using it.

Don't get me wrong; as a mother, I am a part of this vicious cycle of give-and-take with technology and my own child. I continually blame him for his distraction and disconnection due to the technology that I gift-wrapped and gave him for his birthday when he was too young to handle it. All because I worry about him being socially ostracized if he is the only kid without. At his school, he is allowed to take a phone or iPod to have in class to listen to music. Because of our push-pull with technology—he breaks the rules, we take his device away, he earns our trust, he gets it back—he currently does not have any internet-accessing devices in his possession because he was caught watching YouTube skateboarding videos during class. He can't help himself, and he knows it—and so do we. Recognizing the temptation that is his iPod but still wanting to listen to music at school, he found a solution while helping his grandmother clean out her basement—a vintage Walkman! Right now, at school, my son is rocking out to his aunt's '90s cassette tapes, which I find hilarious. When I asked about any social repercussions for being the only kid with a Walkman he responded, "It's embarrassing, but I know it's better than nothing and can't get me in trouble. And . . . it has given me a great appreciation of today's technology and yesterday's lyrics."

Unfortunately, concerns about technology reach far beyond distraction and disconnection. In my experience, among the most worrisome concerns are addiction, amplification, and a whole new set of social norms and expectations.

Addiction

In the past few years, with the young people I have worked with, I have found that some are as addicted to technology, gaming, and social media as they were to nicotine and alcohol in years past. Research confirms what I am seeing. A Common Sense Media report titled *Technology Addiction: Concern, Controversy, and Finding Balance*, notes, "The Common Sense Census, 2015, a representative survey of American tweens (8- to 12-year-olds) and teens (13- to 18-year-olds), documented that outside of school and homework, tweens spend almost six hours per day (5:55 hours) and teens spend almost nine hours per day (8:56 hours) using media." The study dives deeper into internet addiction and internet gaming disorder, stating that "the brains of the identified Internet addicts within several studies resembled those of substance abusers and pathological gamblers." The symptoms of technology addiction look much like those of any addiction: loss of interest in activities that used to bring joy, difficulty sleeping, and a disregard for responsibilities. One of the biggest worries about technology and addiction revolves around the tying of self-worth to scoring, ranking, points, and accomplishments in a virtual world, together with a failure to recognize the passing of time. Does the following conversation sound familiar to you?

> "Zach, how long have you been playing video games?"
> "I don't know . . . maybe an hour? I got back to my room around 2 p.m."
> "Zach, it's 8 p.m. and you missed dinner. You have been playing for six hours."
> "Oh well . . . it was worth it . . . I hit 1,000 in my overall kills."

Unfortunately, this conversation happens all too often when working with young people today, and the unrecognized passage of time when using technology is one of the greatest disrupters to their success.

Amplification

In decades past, when something noteworthy happened at school (a disciplinary incident, a romantic breakup, etc.), the "scandal" would blow over and disappear by the time the next gossip-worthy event happened. Now that smartphones and social media have entered the scene, however, there is no escaping the gossip mill. Every piece of news is amplified, as if broadcast from loudspeakers and plastered on billboards.

So many of the idiotic decisions young people make now come from ideas spread on the internet via YouTube videos, memes, or celebrity challenges. In my recent years working with young people I have responded to emergencies that include burns (freezing boiling water challenge), stomach illness (Tide Pod challenge), broken bones (Keke challenge—dancing beside your car as it continues to drive), and stiches (Kylie Jenner lip challenge). All of these results were inspired by viral videos and challenges popping up on adolescents' social media feeds. The desire to produce a "wow" reaction, to gain followers and popularity, and to one-up the latest viral video are real factors that dictate the decisions many young people are making. What we, the adults, wish to be amplified and celebrated in perpetuity in young people's feeds is not necessarily what they respond to. The world of the next "wow" factor is the technologically amplified reality we need to recognize and navigate in our work with youth.

New Social Norms and Expectations
In Rosalind Wiseman's book *Queen Bees and Wannabes*, she writes about the hierarchy of teenage girls' social networks. Originally published in 2002 and updated in 2016, the book unveils a hidden culture of girls silently agreeing to a set of rituals and rules to live by. Wiseman responds to the common definition of a clique being a group of close friends by saying, "I see it a little differently. I see them as a platoon of soldiers who have banded together because they think this is the best way to survive Girl World. There's a chain of command, and they operate as one to the outside world, even if there may be dissatisfaction within the ranks. Group cohesion is based on unquestionable loyalty to the leaders and an 'it's us against the world' mentality." Add social media to the complicated environment that Wiseman brought to light, and it's clear that the pressure has only grown, with even more rituals and rules that young women must learn and follow in order to survive middle and high school.

Out of the blue, I received an e-mail from two graduates of the Girls' Leadership Camp, asking me if they could return and facilitate a workshop on social media with our middle school campers. "No offense, Brook, but we think the message will be better received coming from someone younger, and with what we are seeing out here, they need it," they told me. I wish I could say, "No offense taken," but ouch! I loved their energy and commitment, and got out of their way to see what they would produce. In the workshop, one leader put up a picture of herself in a bikini holding a strong-woman pose on top of a cliff, about to jump into a pool of water thirty feet below. She asked the group, "What do you think my friends commented on this photo?"

Like a well-rehearsed choir, they started rhyming off exactly what they knew her friends commented: "omg," "goals," "ur so cute," "sexy bod," "gorg," heart heart heart emojis, kissy face kissy face emojis . . . In minutes, these eleven-year-olds had reproduced every comment on her photo. They knew the script.

She then put another photo up on the screen. This time it was her brother in a bathing suit on top of the same cliff doing a strong-man pose, about to jump off into a pool of water thirty feet below. She asked the group, "What do you think my brother's friends commented on his photo?" The girls in the room had no idea. They had never stopped to consider how boys comment on each other's social media. She shared with them the comments: "dude . . . where are you?" "sick bro . . . did you jump?" "whoaaa," "sweet." All their comments were about the location and the adventure, and none addressed his body or attire.

The leader then asked the group, "Why do we do this to ourselves? Why do we complain about people only valuing the way girls and women look and not what we are capable of, or how brilliant we are? And then we turn around and do the exact same thing to each other online? It is time we go back to our friend groups and change the way we celebrate each other." She nailed it, and in her final questions to the group she raised one of my biggest concerns with technology: it makes us feel like we are advancing as a culture, but for the self-esteem of young people, and specifically young women, the script is not new, and may even be causing us to regress.

Porn and Hook-Up Culture

I recognize that many families, schools, and organizations have strong feelings on where, when, with whom—and even if—a discussion about sex should take place. In my experience, confusing messages, as well as misinformation, about sex lead young people to make uninformed and unhealthy choices, choices they may have made differently had their questions been answered by an adult they could confide in and trust to give them straight-talking, informative advice.

Some adults push back, arguing that if we talk about sex, we encourage it. The research tells us this is not the case. The *Guidelines for Comprehensive Sexual Education*, produced by the Sexuality Information and Education Council of the United States, states that, "Research supports a comprehensive approach to sexuality education with numerous studies finding that such programs can help young people delay intercourse, reduce the frequency of intercourse, reduce the number of sexual partners they have, and increase their use of condoms and other contraceptive methods when they do become sexually active."

Young people are going to experiment with acts of a sexual nature, whether or not trusted adults enter into the conversation. From traveling to schools and talking with educators who say that hook-up culture and porn are at the top of their list of concerns, I know that I am not the only one advocating for us to do a better job with conversations about sex. Peggy Orenstein, author of *Girls & Sex*, recently said in an NPR interview that, "Kids are not having intercourse at a younger age, and they're not having more intercourse than they used to. They are engaging in other forms of sexual behavior, younger and more often." Orenstein reports this information after interviewing more than seventy young women between the ages of fifteen and twenty about their attitudes and early experiences with all levels of physical intimacy.

Beyond the concerns of pregnancy and sexually transmitted infections, adults express worry about the emotional impact these other forms of sexual behavior at younger ages are having on youth. I share their concerns, and can confirm that I have seen the negative impact firsthand. On a fall afternoon, an eleventh-grade girl entered my office sobbing and let me know, between tears, that she was feeling extremely left out, rejected, isolated, and alone. These are difficult emotions for a young person (or any person) to navigate. I let her know I was there for her and asked her what I could do to help.

"Well . . . I know you're the dean, and I probably shouldn't share this with you," she started out. "But I also don't know who else to talk to right now. But basically, my friend was gonna hook up with this guy. And the guy Snapchatted her and was like, 'You got a friend you want to invite and we can make it a threesome?' and the girl was like, 'Let me ask around.' And then she asked me, and I have always really wanted to hook up with this guy, and even though I don't really wanna have a threesome, I figured it wouldn't be that weird, and I would still be able to get with the guy, so I said yes. And then when she told him that I would do it, he told her, 'Ew, gross. You gotta find someone else.' And then she told me what he said, and now I just feel totally rejected and embarrassed and alone."

Remember when I told you that life with adolescents is an epic dance party, scary roller coaster, military battlefield, and the warmest hug ever, all mixed into one? This was a scary roller coaster moment. This girl's emotions were so raw and real. She was feeling so rejected and alone. The reasons for these feelings were frightening to me; the hook-up culture and sense that "everyone else was doing it" had become so prevalent and normalized that, although she hesitated slightly to share with me, she came to the conclusion that she wanted to talk about it. With me. The dean.

Cindy Pierce, author of *Sexploitation: Helping Kids Develop Healthy Sexuality in a Porn-Driven World,* shared this in an interview on the influence of porn:

> Internet porn is often the first sexuality educator for young people of all genders and orientations. Boys and men are the biggest consumers of internet porn. In my interviews over the last fifteen years, boys and young men consistently express concern about what they learn in porn and how it doesn't convert to their sexual experiences. Many young women feel like they need to compete with porn. Almost a third of what crosses the internet is porn. The most clicked-on porn becomes the most accessible porn. The excessive sexual violence and aggression directly contributes to consumers' skewed expectations of how bodies appear and respond. Our kids are being pummeled by a tidal wave of hypersexualized messaging; parents and other anchoring adults who engage in conversations about sexuality with their kids early and often stand a chance to become a trusted source for accurate information.

I hear from educators around the country that among their biggest concerns for youth is the combination of sex and technology and the perplexing messages being sent to young people as a result. All the while, the adults who put the technology in the hands of young people are often unwilling to have the conversations that will help them navigate the confusion.

Mental Health and Anxiety

Through my work with schools, camps, and teams, I have witnessed firsthand the debilitating impact anxiety has on young people. Whether they are blanking on a test, walking off the sports field, completely withdrawing, or showing physical symptoms and having full-on panic attacks, students manifest anxiety in many different ways.

In an article published in the *Journal of Developmental and Behavioral Pediatrics*, titled "Epidemiology and Impact of Health-care Provider Diagnosed Anxiety and Depression among US Children," researchers found that, as of 2011–2012, more than one in twenty—or 2.6 million—US children aged six to seventeen years had current anxiety or depression that had previously been diagnosed by a health-care provider. Another important statistic: at the time of this study, approximately one in five children with current anxiety and depression had not received mental health treatment in the past year. The National Alliance on Mental Illness reports that LGBTQ individuals are almost three times more likely than others to experience a mental health condition such as major depression or generalized anxiety disorder. The Anxiety and Depression Association of America provides research that shows untreated children with anxiety disorders are at higher risk of performing poorly in school, missing out on important social experiences, and abusing alcohol or illicit substances.

We know the statistics, and many of us have had the experience of supporting a child coping with anxiety or other mental health illnesses. When teachers bring up mental health and anxiety as one of their top three concerns facing young people today, it is partly because they fear the impact of the disorder on the child, and partly because it is extremely difficult to know what to do when one of the young people in your care is struggling. We are educators, music teachers, camp counselors, coaches, and youth directors, not mental health experts. But often in our work with young people we are launched into roles we are not entirely prepared for.

Complicating the treatment of mental health is the importance of parents and other trusted adults agreeing on the best approach with the young person battling the disorder. Often, a young person with anxiety comes with parents who have anxiety too. Children with parents who have anxiety are two to seven times more likely to develop an anxiety disorder, according to Golda Ginsburg, a psychiatry professor at UConn Health, as reported in a 2015 NPR article titled "Parents Can Learn How to Prevent Anxiety in Their Children."

Lynn Lyons, author of *Anxious Kids, Anxious Parents* and my favorite speaker on the topic of anxiety, says, "The way you learn how to manage life is by making mistakes or by stepping into things that feel uncertain, uncomfortable, or overwhelming and then proving to yourself through experience that you can manage it." According to Lyons, schools fall into the trap of providing accommodations for students with no weaning-off plan; creating "escapes" that are warm, safe, and cozy, which inadvertently supports the anxiety and avoidance; and working toward removing the anxiety altogether by giving young people special schedules, warnings, and other modifications to their day. These actions, which Lyons says unintentionally feed the disorder, are what feels most natural for a caring adult to do when watching a young person struggle. Who would think that creating a warm and cozy escape could actually be harmful for an anxious child, and not what is most helpful?

The growing number of young people struggling with mental health issues confirms our concern for this risk and its impact. I believe it rises to the top of the concern list for trusted adults because the symptoms—missing class or practice, refusing to engage, breaking down in tears, and so on—can disrupt and distract from the work we set out to do, and our responsibilities surrounding mental health can feel confusing and heavy. We know that our reactions are important, and the way we handle a young person in these sensitive moments can help alter this young person's future. Walking this thin line, and wanting to do what is right by the child, is an ongoing concern for adults who work with young people.

Supposed-To Syndrome

Looking at the big list of risky behaviors and consequences, as well the top three concerns of (1) technology and social media, (2) porn and hook-up culture, and (3) mental health and anxiety, which I hear about over and over again from educators, I see a core problem that I believe lies at the heart of all these issues. It's something I call "Supposed-To Syndrome."

In my workshops with young people, specifically those of high school age, I ask them who they think they are supposed to be. Silence. "Supposed to" as determined by who, the participants typically want to know. Great question! And a complicated one. Rather than answer it, I ask them to draw: "Draw what and who you believe you are supposed to be, based on the messages you get from all sources in your life." I provide a piece of paper with an androgynous body outline and some markers, and they get to work.

The pieces of art students produce show remarkable insight into the confusion raging in the teenage brain. Quite often, they begin by changing the body outline. Over the past ten years, I have watched the body morphing shift, particularly on the girls' papers, from Taylor Swift–like bodies to Kardashian-style bodies, from a high school female body that is "supposed to be" thin to one that is "supposed to be" curvy, all in one decade.

I also see conflict on the page. I see participants represent in illustration what their peers expect them to be/look/act like versus what their parents expect versus what their college advisor promotes versus what pop culture approves. I have watched them chop the body into quarters and eighths, with each piece representing a different identity they need to wear throughout their day in order to gain approval from the group of people they are currently with. From a body sporting ripped abs and expensive sneakers to one adorned in the latest fashion and accessorized by a tiny dog in a carrier, to one surrounded by books and wearing a Harvard sweater—most of the figures complemented with displays of the newest technology and millions of followers and admirers—the participants draw it all.

At one school, I encountered something I had never seen. Tasked with empowering the female leaders of the school to step up and start making positive change, I started our two-hour evening workshop by asking all forty girls to draw what they are "supposed to be" as high school juniors and seniors. What I witnessed as they drew was pretty standard, typical of what I saw from the students in most places I visited. At the end, when they shared their images, however, there was one baffling similarity from page to page, and it was something I had not seen before. Every single image had a cake, cookie, or pie drawn with an X over it, or some indication on their paper that desserts were forbidden. I was so curious, first, because I love desserts. And second, because I wanted to know how it could be that forty out of forty girls drew the same figure on their papers. When I asked about it, one girl spoke up. Here is how our conversation went, in front of all forty girls:

"Well . . . there is this Wellness Committee at school, who is looking out for the wellness of students," she said.

"Is it a student committee?" I asked.

"No, it's all adults. And they decided that the location of the dessert table was in a bad spot because people were grabbing dessert and eating it while they were waiting in line for the salad bar or hot food. So they moved the dessert table to the other side of the dining hall."

"Okay. Do you agree with that decision?"

"Yes and no. I agree it was a good idea to move it. I don't agree with where they put it, because it is right by where the boys' lacrosse team eats lunch. And, at least, from my own experience I know they have been making rude comments when girls get desserts."

"What kind of rude comments?"

"When I went and got cookies, one of them called me a pig."

"Really?"

"Well, no . . . not exactly . . . it was more like he said it with his eyes."

In this moment, Supposed-to Syndrome felt stronger than ever. One girl had one experience that she perceived and shared with other girls, and the idea that girls don't eat dessert spread across the school in an instant, becoming what girls at this school are supposed to do.

We threw out the rest of the agenda and got to work writing a proposal, as a group of empowered female leaders, to add students to the Wellness Committee and to reassess the location of the dessert table. This was not the type of positive change I had set out to inspire that evening, but in observing and listening to the need, it was clear that the dessert table in this school had become a concrete issue that should be tackled if the girls were to combat Supposed-To Syndrome. The workshop gave them a forum for talking about their thoughts and an opportunity to step up. I could also now add Advocate of Access to Desserts for All to my résumé!

Young people are impressionable. Their stories tell us so, and the research confirms it.

Frances E. Jensen, author of *The Teenage Brain*, a book I have relied on heavily since it was published in 2015, notes that the teenage brain is a "double whammy—a jacked-up stimulus-seeking brain not yet fully capable of making mature decisions." She goes on to say that this double whammy "hits teens pretty hard, and the consequences to them, and their families, can sometimes be catastrophic." Adolescents seek activities and interactions with high emotional charge, but they don't yet have the full set of skills necessary to handle them. Dr. Jensen writes:

This is why adolescence is a time of true wonder. Because of the flexibility and growth of the brain, adolescents have a window of opportunity with an increased capacity for remarkable accomplishments. But flexibility, growth, and exuberance are a double-edged sword because an "open" and excitable brain also can be adversely affected by stress, drugs, chemical substances, and any number of changes in the environment. And because of an adolescent's often overactive brain, those influences can result in problems dramatically more serious than they are for adults.

The multitude of messages coming at young people from their parents, teachers, friends and from their wider social environment and pop culture—often via their always-on phones—leaves them confused and with blurred values and little sense of self. I imagine young people as having one hundred tiny speakers all around their heads, like a halo. Messages, often contradictory ones, pummel them all day, confusing them and preventing them from developing a strong sense of self. Every day, they are grappling with the following questions:

Who am I?
Who do others think I am?
Who do others want me to be?
Who do I want to be?

Calibrating their inner compass and facing the clash of identities are necessary tasks adolescents must tackle as they push on toward adulthood. Who will influence the way young people answer these questions, and how these influencers will make their mark, is largely up to us, the trusted adults. We are now well aware of the symptoms, risks, worries, concerns and problems facing young people today. Now, let's discuss the solution.

CHAPTER 3

Why Trusted Adults Matter

Whatever risky behaviors or symptoms of Supposed-To Syndrome we see in young people, the answer to their positive growth, on-target development, and overall health is always the same: the presence in their lives of a trusted adult.

A report titled *The Science of Resilience* by the National Scientific Council on the Developing Child, a multidisciplinary collaboration chaired by Harvard Graduate School of Education's Jack Shonkoff, poses the question and answer this way: "Why do some children adapt and overcome, while others bear lifelong scars that flatten their potential? A growing body of evidence points to one common answer: Every child who winds up doing well has had at least one stable and committed relationship with a supportive adult." Whether the obstacles to overcome are technology and social media, pornography and hook-up culture, mental health issues and anxiety, or another risk or combination of risks, the greatest preventative factor is a consistent, reliable, present, and trusted adult. This adult has to be important enough for a young person to want to make proud, or even better, perhaps, important enough that they do not want to disappoint. Fortunately, many young people grow up with trusted adults in their home in the form of parents and guardians. Some, however, do not. Regardless of whether there is a trusted adult in the household, growing research tells us that a relationship with a trusted adult outside the home has enormous significance on the development of youth.

A 2013 study by Child Trends in Bethesda, Maryland, titled *Caring Adults: Important for Child Well-Being*, shared the following key findings:

1. Children and adolescents who have a formal or informal "mentor-like" relationship with someone outside their home are less likely to have externalizing behavior problems (bullying) and internalizing problems (depression).

2. This group is also more likely to complete tasks they start, remain calm in the face of challenges, show interest in learning new things, volunteer in the community, engage in physical activities, participate in out-of-school time activities, and be engaged in school.

The case for the presence of trusted adults, outside the home, in the lives of young people is strong. The research confirms it, but we, as educators, camp counselors, and coaches know it from firsthand experiences. We have all seen different results and behaviors from the young people we work with based on the types of relationships they had with the adults surrounding them, and we have our own stories of the ways trusted adults have impacted and shaped our own personal growth and development.

Your Trusted Adults

If we are interested in being trusted, reliable adults for young people, we need to reflect first on who, if anyone, was there for us. Take a moment and think back to the person you were when you were the age of the young people you work with.

Did you have a trusted adult in your life?
Who was that person?
What characteristics and strengths did this person possess?
Did this person know they were your trusted adult?
How did you know you could trust them?

In the trainings I facilitate, I have been told about the most amazing family members, teachers, coaches, drama club leaders, youth pastors, employers, neighbors, and music instructors who made an incredible impact on the participants. The adults taking part in these trainings are now paying it forward as trusted adults in the lives of the young people they work with, and they describe beautifully what the adults in their lives did for them, how they spoke to them, and, more importantly, how they listened to them.

It is not uncommon, however, to find many people in the room who did not have a trusted adult in their lives when they were in middle or high school. In one training, a school principal looked at me, a little teary, and said, "This exercise was really hard for me. Middle school was really hard for me, and I'm not sure I fully thought about that until now. I really didn't have anyone I could trust. Do you think that is why I have dedicated my life to being a reliable adult presence for middle schoolers?"

I couldn't answer that question, but I think he did. One of the top tactics for doing our best work with young people is pausing to assess our motivations: Why is this work important to us? How does it connect to our own journey, our own story?

Personally, I was fortunate to have so many trusted adults I could hardly count them. As an oldest child, I sought the approval, admiration, and advice of anyone older than me. There were people I babysat for, local lifeguards, school secretaries, softball coaches, teachers, hockey coaches, and a number of family members, including my parents, who I trusted and who I believed had my best interest in mind.

Being a trusted adult is a big responsibility, but it's also something that comes naturally to those who are generally nurturing human beings. Often, when we fall short, it is the expectations of the job—the pressure to have students deliver high test scores, a winning season, or the perfect school musical—that distract us from our real work, which is helping young people become the happy, healthy adults they want to be.

What if I asked you this: Is the primary responsibility outlined in your job description (teaching algebra, coaching the soccer team, putting on the senior play) *truly* your primary responsibility? Is it possible that your official primary responsibility is just an avenue for you to do your *real* work, which is caring for, guiding, and advising young people? I'm not, of course, saying that algebra is not important. It is. But I do believe if the real work of nurturing humans doesn't get done, then there's no hope for the algebra.

Your Job Description

Here is an exercise for you: List your priorities in your work with young people—what are you really hoping to teach them? Think about the ways you are evaluated in your role. Very likely, your evaluation is based on students' test scores and grades or wins and losses rather than on the human connection you make with your students and players. Think about the way your progress with a young person is evaluated by the organization you work for; is the health and safety of the young people in your care part of your review? Now, take your current job description and rewrite it. Write your job description to include what, how, and why you approach your work with young people the way you do.

After one of my trainings, a woman asked to speak with me. She wanted to share a story. We found a quiet place, and she began: "You're right. You're right, Brook. Algebra is the avenue, not the destination. I have taught social studies for the past twenty-five years. I am retiring this year. I almost didn't come to your training tonight because, I figured, what is left for me to learn in my twenty-fifth year of teaching social studies to middle schoolers? But my friend dragged me here because we are going for a glass of wine after this! And I'm sorry that's what it took to get me here, but I am so glad I came."

"It's nice to know that wine got you here, and not my headshot or compelling workshop description!" I answered.

The teacher continued, "I have been at the same school for all twenty-five years. This means I have had the pleasure and pain of watching generations of the same family grow through our school. I say pleasure because it is great to get to know families, to teach a child and then teach their children. And I say pain, because it is difficult to watch unhealthy patterns run through a family generation after generation and not be able to do anything about it. But just the other day, I went into a local coffee shop in a town nearby and I was greeted by a young woman behind the counter who said, 'Mrs. O'Neill?'"

The teacher took a deep breath to compose herself as she described the exchange.

"Lucy?"

"Yes! It's me, Mrs. O'Neill! Look at me! Full-time job. I'm a manager."

Mrs. O'Neill told me the history of this young woman's life, her struggles. She'd suffered trauma in her childhood, and with substance abuse, early pregnancy, and a variety of other concerns surrounding her, it was all too likely she would become a victim of her circumstances. Because Mrs. O'Neill had witnessed the choices and life paths of Lucy's family members, she always worried deeply for Lucy. But here was Lucy. Smiling, proud, about twenty-three years old, wearing her uniform and ecstatic to see her middle school social studies teacher.

"Wow, I am so proud of you, Lucy! This is fantastic. It is so wonderful to see you so happy and so successful."

"I am independent and I am strong, and it is all thanks to you," Lucy said.

"I'm not sure I can take that much credit, Lucy."

"Well, you should. You saved my life. I have always wanted to write you a letter, and I am sorry I haven't. But I am so happy you came in here today so I can thank you. Do you remember the eighth-grade hiking trip?"

"Of course. We do it every year."

"Do you remember what you said to me?"

"I can't say that I do."

"I was really struggling and did not want to hike anymore. I kept saying, 'Look at how much we have left to climb,' and you said, 'Lucy, stop looking at how much you have left to climb and look at how much you have already climbed. In life, too, it's okay to look back and take pride in what you have accomplished, and remind yourself how powerful and strong you are before you tackle what's ahead.'"

"I said that?"

"Yes, Mrs. O'Neill. You said that. We finished the hike too. And when I got home I wrote that in my journal. Now, every time I have to do something difficult or that I'm nervous about, or that I just don't want to do, I go back and read that. I read it before I interviewed for this job. Your words saved my life."

Mrs. O'Neill had tears in her eyes at this point in her story. Reflecting on her twenty-five years of teaching, she didn't know if she had really made an impact. She honestly had hoped that more of her students would become educators and then write her letters describing how her class, her curriculum, had changed their lives.

"How could it be that I changed someone's life through my job, but well outside of my job description? Saying something I don't even remember? And saying it on a mountain, not even in my classroom! So . . . you're right, Brook. Social studies is the avenue, not the destination. The real work happens in and around the other work."

A trusted adult relationship is the solution to life's problems for so many young people. They may not show it (they may not even know it), but they crave the attention and respect of the adults around them. They are eager to feel seen, heard, and worthy. We teachers, coaches, program directors spend hours planning exciting and challenging curricula, balanced practice plans, excursions, adventures, and activities, but often it is the time we spend on the fringes of that work that has the greatest impact.

Didn't I Just Say That?

If children's parents are present in their lives, of course we hope they are trusted adults for their children. I would argue, however, that a parent's effectiveness is placed on hold for a period of time as a young person naturally prepares to launch into full adolescence and, eventually, adulthood. I say this with full authority, as a parent who has been, at times, placed on hold by her child.

My son had just been suspended from school for attempting to purchase a vape pen. When he was caught, school officials searched his locker and found another vape pen in his Harry Potter lunch box. I repeat, his *Harry Potter lunch box*. Old enough to vape, but still sleeping with a teddy bear and taking his lunch to school in a Harry Potter lunch box. If this isn't a perfect demonstration of the teenage brain, I don't know what is.

Here's the whole story: On a whim, I had decided to take a break from work and get out of the house, so I walked the dogs up the road to meet my son at the bus stop. This was not a regular habit of mine, but it wasn't terribly out of the ordinary either. As I turned the corner and yelled, "Heyyyy!" my son jumped about four feet in the air, fell to his knees, and then acted more excited to see me and the dogs than ever before. My senses tingled—something was up. Or was he just this excited to see me on a random Tuesday in January?

As we walked back to the house together he said, "Hey Mom, it doesn't seem like we have gotten the mail recently, why don't I walk back up to the mailbox and get it for you?" This boy does not volunteer to walk anywhere, ever. Something was definitely up.

"We have to get to drum lessons, so there's no time. Hop in the car—let's go."

We had a great time. We sang, laughed, chatted. Nothing seemed out of the normal routine, until our ride home.

"Hey, Mom . . . it has been really nice that you and Dad have been driving me to the bus stop in the morning because it has been so cold, but I have been a little groggy in school recently, so I am thinking a brisk walk in the morning might do me some good. I think I'll walk to the bus stop tomorrow." Did I mention this boy does not willingly walk anywhere? And he most certainly doesn't use the word "brisk." What was going on? The only thing I could think of was that he might have dropped something in the road that he wanted to get, but didn't want me to know about. But what could it be?

So I asked him, "Did you drop something in the road earlier that you need to get?"

"No." Stone face.

I drove slowly, very slowly, onto our dirt road that only three other cars use in the winter. I saw something blue and shiny in the road where I had startled him earlier. I put the car in park, with the headlights shining on it.

"Are you sure you didn't drop something in the road?"

Stone face.

Dramatically, with the *Law & Order* theme song playing in my head, I got out of the car and walked toward the object. A vape pen. I picked it up, held it up, and looked back at the car, knowing he could see me though I could not see him, and I struck my best, "Oh really . . . then what is this?!" stance. It was one of my finer mothering moments. A feeling of "gotcha" came over me, followed by a tidal wave of real parent feelings: complete disappointment and major concern.

I got back in the car, and did not have words, so I didn't say anything. We sat in silence for a moment, before he broke it with something other than the apology I was looking for. "Why does my mom have to know all this stuff? Nobody else's parents would even know what that was. I can't get away with anything." Tears. More spewing of frustration. More tears.

Many conversations, lots of education, and concrete consequences followed. Two weeks later, I saw a message come across his iPod from a kid he likes to snowboard with, "Dude . . . did you get it?" My senses tingled again.

When I asked my son what the young man was referring to, he gave me a guilty-looking "I don't know."

We sat at the bus stop (because, of course, now he wanted rides again—so much for the brisk morning walk!), and I said, "I don't know the boy messaging you. I trust you to make good friends who have your best interest in mind. His message felt to me like he was asking you to buy, steal, or borrow something for him, and I am worried. I hope you know better than to risk your character and reputation for someone else. Remember that anything that happens at school related to substance would be suspendable, and your grades are already in a tough spot right now."

"Mom, I am well aware. I would never do something like that."

"Listen, I hate to assume anything bad, but we did just have the vape incident, and I . . ."

"Mom, I get it."

Would you believe that at that moment my son, while reassuring me that he would never do anything like that, had in his left pocket the original vape pen (which my husband thought I'd disposed of and I thought he had disposed of, and which our son had stolen back out of my pocket) and in his right pocket $60 taken from my dresser—his Christmas money from his aunt, earmarked for a guitar strap—which he planned to take to school so he could purchase another vape pen?

Eight hours later, the principal called me.

"Your son is being suspended for purchasing a vape pen from another student, as well as having possession of another vape pen. It was found in his Harry Potter lunch box."

Growing brains, growing pains.

There was so much to unpack here. So much to understand and sort out. So much to tell him. Of course, as parents, you question where you have gone wrong, what you haven't told him, what you haven't shown him. Is he not busy enough? Is he happy? Are his needs being met? On and on and on . . . you question your decisions and worry about his future.

Our son's health and well-being were at stake, and we were especially taken aback by the fact that he had no idea what chemical substance was in the liquid he was inhaling. But among my husband's concerns was our child's poor business skills: "So you're telling me, this kid asked you to buy something for him, you did not get money from him, instead you fronted your money, gave it to another kid, getting nothing in return, and now you lost $60 and got suspended? This sounds like a terrible business deal right from the start."

Beyond business advice, my husband shared the following truth bomb: "You are the company you keep. Is purchasing a vape pen a determining factor of the rest of your life? Not necessarily, but being a kid who vapes will determine the type of people you hang out with, and those people will determine how your network grows, and that determines what is right and wrong, good and bad, celebrated and ridiculed. The people you start spending time with now could have a huge impact on what direction your life goes."

My husband was describing Supposed-To Syndrome perfectly. We choose our own surroundings and decide whose expectations we are going to meet—we create our own "supposed to's."

We were met with more stone face and little response. It did not feel like anything we did or said was getting through. Consequences included losing snowboarding privileges, theater, and his iPod for a long period of time, with a well-outlined and challenging plan to earn it all back. Lucky for us, there was a huge snowstorm the week of his suspension, and shoveling filled his days. Our neighborhood has never had such clean porches and walkways in January.

I let his drum teacher, Jared, know that he had been suspended and wouldn't make it to his lesson that week. Jared pushed back, asking if he could know why. I shared the story, and Jared responded, "Instead of taking it away, can we double his lessons this week? I think I might be able to help." He told me that he had faced some struggles in high school and asked if it was okay for him to share with my son. Feeling like we needed all the help we could get, I told him to go for it.

My son returned home after his drum lesson that week, and when we asked how it went, here is what he said: "It was awesome. Jared shared with me some really important information about vaping and smoking. He told me his life story. He also told me that this choice doesn't define who I am, but it can determine the type of people I will end up surrounding myself with. And that can end up defining me. So . . . I need to really think about who I want to be, and then I need to surround myself with people like that. Jared just really gets me."

I thought my husband's head was going to explode, "Isn't that almost exactly what I said to you?"

"Uh . . . I don't think so. Did you say something like that?"

I interrupted this exchange to save them both. Because of my research and training on trusted adults, I knew exactly what was happening here. My husband, a tech salesperson who doesn't work with adolescents other than our own, couldn't see it. We had been placed on hold.

"Bill," I told him privately, "we used to be the jelly beans, now we're the brussels sprouts."

"What are you talking about?" he questioned.

"In Lisa Damour's book *Untangled*, she described this phenomenon perfectly. In adolescence, parents go from being the jelly beans to the brussels sprouts. We might be good for him, but we are not what he wants right now. His drum teacher gets to be the jelly beans, and we are stuck being the brussels sprouts."

"I make great brussels sprouts . . ."

"I know, Bill, I know . . ."

To be honest, however, as I coached my husband through this, I was in need of some support too. I was used to being in the role of the trusted adult, not the parent partnering with the trusted adult. This was a difficult moment for me. My son was beginning to seek advice, information, and guidance elsewhere. It is painful to accept that someone else might be more effective than we are with our child for a certain period of their life. But we know it's true. We did it to our parents, and our parents did it to their parents. We had reached a natural step in our son's preparations to fly the nest.

The job of the parent is to surround the child with people like you: adults who have strong values and the child's best interest in mind. Professionals who know how to build trust with young people while maintaining healthy and clear boundaries. Adults like Jared, who know that drums are an avenue and not the destination.

So . . . here we go. In the next chapters, we will dive into best practices you can use to build trust with young people, and ways that organizations can set up their teams to do the same.

CHAPTER 4

Building Trust in Everyday Moments

Years ago, an article found its way into my inbox from the *Huffington Post* called, "How to Talk to Little Girls." As someone who identified as a girl/woman myself, and as the founder and director of a Girls' Leadership Camp, I figured I could not possibly learn anything from this article. Instead, I hoped to have the work I was doing validated. When the article shared criticisms toward adults for immediately rhyming off comments to young girls that solely focus on "how darn cute/pretty/beautiful/well-dressed/well-manicured/well-coiffed they are," I paused. I had performed in that exact scene that morning when I saw my friend's four-year-old daughter. "What a pretty dress you are wearing!" I exclaimed.

How could this be? With all of my training, my values, my mission, and all that I see, how could I immediately have placed importance and value on this child's attire rather than her intelligence, interests, and achievements? I could have asked anything: "What is your favorite song? Movie? Book? How high can you jump? How fast can you run? Can you count to ten with me?" I had not seen this girl since she was two, and my instinct, in our brief meeting, was to do the easy thing, the less empowering thing, and compliment her appearance.

As disappointed as I was in myself, I was grateful for the message and the reminder. I could do better, and in the future I would do better. Even when we are the best of the best in our roles, and feel confident in the way we work with young people, there is always room for growth, improvement, and reminders. The baseline duty we can fulfill as adults is showing up for young people and just being there for them. The way we show up, and the thought we put into our words and actions, however, can have an outsize influence on their development.

When I ask people how they knew they could trust certain adults when they were two, twelve, or twenty years old, the nearly universal answer is, "They were just there for me." Youth—and adults—naturally seek the feeling that someone is in their corner. Just being there isn't as simple as it looks, however. Our reliable presence might be what we project to the young people in our care, and we know it's working if they feel that we're "just there for them." But like a good play, a great game, or a well-delivered speech, a ton of behind-the-scenes work and practice is what makes the result look effortless. We need to train and talk about what it means to just be there, and we all need reminders and reinforcements that focus us on the everyday ways we can build trusting relationships and keep the important things at the center of our attention. Whether it's our verbal language, our body language, our approach, or our timing, there are many factors that can make or break the trust we need to build in order to make the impact we want.

Declaring Motive

"Why do you care?" This is the most common (and most annoying!) question middle and high schoolers today ask of the adults in their lives. It can follow almost any statement or question an adult directs at them:

"You're out of dress code." "Why do you care?"
"Did you get enough to eat for lunch?" "Why do you care?"
"What kind of music are you listening to these days?" "Why do you care?"
"When is your next home game?" "Why do you even care?"

As much as we want to roll our eyes and say, "When you respond that way you are waving a giant red flag on top of a giant mountain, indicating that something is going on with you and you are in deep need of a trusted adult's attention right now!" we don't say this. If we did, the young person would sprint away from us faster than a track star. Instead, we take a moment, we breathe, and we ask ourselves where we want to go with this conversation.

My go-to line, any time a student needs reassurance about why I care to address a concern, show interest, or ask a question, is: "It is my job as an adult in your life to care about your health, happiness, safety, and success, and I am committed to this job."

On one occasion a young man frantically entered my office and dropped an unexpected information bomb on my desk. Here is how the conversation went:

"I just feel the need to tell you this, and I hope you will do something about it because it is wrong and bad."

"Take a seat, Chris, let's talk."

"I can't now. I just need you to know that Mr. Johnson smokes pot. And he told me about it. And I think he should be fired."

Chris then exited my office at the same frantic pace he had entered.

One day later, Chris came to my office again, agitated, and before I could even end my phone call he said, "Why is he still here?"

I shared with Chris that I had immediately reported the information to our Human Resources department and they were looking into it. It was certainly a matter I believed would be addressed, and it was out of my hands and in the hands of those properly trained to handle it.

My concerns for Chris were growing. I scheduled a meeting with Chris and his advisor during a free block, so he couldn't fly out of my office.

"Chris, I just want to check in on how you are doing. What's going on?"

"Why do you even care?" he said waving his giant "I'm in need" red flag on top of his giant "I'm in need" mountain.

"It's my job as an adult in your life to care about your health, happiness, safety, and success. I am committed to this job and want to check in with you on all areas of your school life."

Tears.

His advisor and I sat in silence while Chris sobbed.

He slowly opened up and shared that Mr. Johnson had been sending him inappropriate e-mails. He had trusted this teacher, shared interests with him, and really enjoyed their time together, but things had taken an uncomfortable turn. Chris did not want to upset his teacher, but was also terrified and mortified to be receiving the messages. So, instead of confronting the issue that was really bothering him, he shared with me that Mr. Johnson smokes pot, hoping that this teacher would be fired.

It makes perfect sense. Chris knew he needed help but he also thought he could save himself embarrassment by taking care of the situation himself. He couldn't—nor should he be expected to. As he heard me say we cared about him, and saw his advisor nodding along and confirming his care, he chose to trust us. He found confidence in believing that we had his best interest at heart and would do anything in our power to help him. But we had to tell him, to say explicitly that we were there to help, before he could even consider accepting our help and choosing to trust us.

In these moments when we reveal our intentions, we make a big school small. We create the feeling of a school made for one. We encourage players to understand that, although they are a part of a team, they are still individuals with individual needs. A young person's mental and physical health; their level of happiness and the things that bring them happiness; their safety and what allows them to feel safe; and their success as they define it, are unique to them. Young people need to know we are there for them, and they need to know *why* we are there for them.

Hitting the Mark

Like learning what motivates people, learning to guide others in setting goals takes practice, and looks different with every individual. In my roles as teacher, camp director, and coach, I have seen it all and can place adolescent goal setters into two categories: those who aim too high and those whose targets are too low. There is a type of "Goldilocks" teenager who gets it just right but this is a rare breed, and these individuals have usually built their skills through much self-reflection, failure, success, and, typically, observation of older siblings. All styles of goal setters function in their own way to stay on track and head toward their goals. As adults, we need to explore the best ways to work with them.

The "Aim-Too-Highers"

For a long time, I struggled with how to work with an aim-too-high kind of goal setter. Was I supposed to be the reality check? Was it my job to burst the balloon of the 4-foot, 11½-inch, 110-pound hockey-obsessed ninth-grader who believed he was going to make the varsity team? Should I tell the tone-deaf girl with the crackling voice that odds were low she would make it onto *The Voice* and emerge as America's next pop superstar?

No. The answer is no, and I learned this from a student. Jenny was an advisee of mine who dreamed of attending Princeton University. She knew, I knew, and her parents knew that this was not a realistic option. My biggest fear, however, was that she would stand up at her Princeton graduation one day, wave her diploma, and say, "This is for you, Mrs. Raney. You didn't believe I could do it, but here I am, I did it." So I stepped back and asked myself, how can I have an honest conversation with Jenny without crushing her dreams?

I started with, "I believe in you, and I think it's always important to ask, what happens if you don't get into Princeton?"

She responded: "For me, it's like when I go for a run on the treadmill. I can set a goal to run two miles, knowing I can run two miles. Or, I can set a goal to run six miles. I know I can't run six miles, but if I aim for it, I might get to four miles. And four miles is better than two miles, right? It's the same thing for college. If I aim for Princeton, knowing the chances are small that I will actually get to Princeton, I know there will probably be a pretty good place for me on the way there."

She sold me! It was not my style of goal setting, but I needed to let go of that to best support her. While I feared a letdown for Jenny if she didn't meet her goal, she only viewed the goal as an aspiration that would push her to stretch herself. My job was to remind her of this, and to continue to support the dream.

I hear students complain about their teachers saying, "You can be anything" or their guidance counselors hanging posters with messages like, "Shoot for the moon, even if you miss you will land among the stars." But what would they rather the adults in their lives say? "Don't bother trying too hard because your destiny is already determined by your race, gender, or socioeconomic status"? I have learned to embrace the positivity of the aim-too-highers, to grab hold of the string of their optimism balloon and join them on their float. It is the job of the trusted adult to help them pursue their dreams with one eye looking out for a soft landing place. We must consistently check in on the small goals that lead to the big goals, and that keep us both tethered to a real plan.

The shadow side of "too high" goal setting is a "toss all my eggs in one basket" mentality. What do we do with the young man who expects to be the next Jay-Z and therefore blows off his coursework? Or the student who plans to take over the family business someday so none of this other stuff matters? Or the one who is told by his own parents that he is destined to play NHL hockey, so there is no room for any non-hockey-related activities in his life? I have found success in asking students to identify the skills that Jay-Z needs to be Jay-Z, that adults need to run a family business, and that pro athletes need in order to balance the demands of their jobs and lives. When asked this question, the students returned well-rounded lists of skills. Through this exercise, they recognize that successful people in any area of life, from stay-at-home parent to corporate CEO, need social-emotional skills, grit and resilience, time-management skills, a strong work ethic, and the list goes on. Specific physics formulas might not be directly transferable to the goal, but certainly the ability to learn and the discipline to stick with a difficult task are.

One summer, a camper stated in a workshop that "My goal is to be the first female president of the United States, and if I don't reach that goal, I will probably just be secretary of state or something."

Although the goal of becoming president or secretary of state is noble and amazing, as a realist I was tempted to let this "aim-too-higher" know that there are lots of other places her leadership is needed as well, and what an honor it is to also serve at the community, county, and state levels. I stopped myself, however, remembered the path to Princeton, and instead replied, "You go, girl! Let's make a list of the small goals you are going to have to achieve, and all the skills you will need to learn, on the way to your big goal."

The "Think-Too-Smallers"

I love working with students and players who think too small, aim too low, and who believe they are capable of less than the adults around them believe. This job entails opening their eyes and showing them their own possibilities.

In my early years as an educator, a student of mine filled out a goal sheet and wrote "C's for me." I was taken aback. Plenty of C's showed up on my transcripts as a high school student, but you wouldn't find them on my goal sheets. I had high expectations for myself, and although I sometimes bumped up against the reality of my academic limitations, I was always going to aim for A's. When I urged this student to aim higher (without asking questions first), I accidently implied that his goal wasn't good enough. Knowing what I know now, I should not have placed judgment on another person's goal or definition of success. As an educator or advisor, I get to guide, prod, push, pull, support, leverage, and expose, but it is not my place to judge.

My student told me, "I wrote down 'C's for me' because I have been a C student my whole life. I have never gotten support in my learning until now. I do think I can do better, but I am scared to write it down. I will be upset if I don't reach my goal, and if I do better than my goal I will be happy. So, a safe goal for me is C's."

A safe goal is a far cry from shooting for the moon, but his logic made sense. His way of setting goals motivated him. Small victories every day energized him, while falling short of his goal would have demoralized an already underconfident student. I had to meet him in a different place than my other advisees. My job was to celebrate the small victories with him, and assist him in reshaping his identity surrounding school. For each grade he was satisfied with, we debriefed the habits and actions that got him there. With each setback, we reset and reinforced that one grade does not define an entire academic reputation.

Goal Setter ID

Four questions to help identify the type of goal setter you are working with:

1. What is a goal you set in the past? Did you achieve it? How?
2. How do you define success for you?
3. If you achieve your goals, what do you do next?
4. If you do not achieve your goals, what do you do next?

Using the information gathered from these questions and the stories in the text, determine the type of goal setter you believe you are working with: an "Aim-Too-Higher," a "Think-Too-Smaller," or a rare "Goldilocks."

"Aim-Too-Higher": Shoots for the moon, even though—whether they know it or not—it is well out of reach. Motivated by big aspirations. Will still be satisfied (or learn to be satisfied) when achieving lower than the goal.

"Goldilocks": Through failure and success, has learned to set goals "just right." Picks a path, makes a plan, and heads toward a realistic, achievable, and slightly challenging goal. Motivated by setting a specific goal and achieving it.

"Think-Too-Smaller": Sets the bar low in order to achieve. Motivated by consistently achieving goals, even if they are not overly challenging. Will be satisfied when results surpass goals set.

Read the definitions of the types of goal setters to the young people you are working with and have a discussion about the type of goal setter they believe they are. If your labels agree, share how you believe you can best support them, and, of course, ask them how they believe you can best support them in pursuing their goals. If your labels don't agree, continue the conversation to learn more about how they feel they can be supported.

Write It Down

Many goal-setting models exist, designed to help us define our purpose and stay on track. My preferred method is the SMART model—the acronym stands for specific, measurable, agreed upon, realistic, and time based. Project Smart provides a tried-and-true framework that can be adjusted for individuals and groups, helping everyone from students to businesspeople articulate their goals and define the objectives needed to get them there. In my work, I have found that asking a young person about the goals they have for their summer, school year, or even for a class can return a huge variety of answers, and does not always provide the common ground or directional advice I was seeking. A framework like SMART or a pre-lesson in goal setting can help get everyone on the same page about the types of goals that will be most helpful.

It is also important to establish what success will look like, by identifying and understanding the young person's values. Goals should not be one dimensional, and they shouldn't be too broad or complicated either. If you ask a person to set goals that relate only to school or sports, you are making a value judgment about what is important. Separating goals into categories such as mind, body, and spirit can inspire conversation and remind young people you see them as more than just students or athletes. Before setting goals and writing them out, ask your students to consider all aspects of their lives:

- What goals do you have surrounding the care and growth of your mind?
  (curiosities, reading, exploration, academics, knowledge, mindfulness, and focus)
- What goals do you have surrounding the care and growth of your body?
  (physical self-care, development of physical strength, endurance, and skills)
- What goals do you have surrounding the care and growth of your spirit?
  (religion/spirituality, community, service, leadership, social life, emotions, family and relationships)

Many of the goals in the arenas of mind, body, and spirit will overlap, but asking about all these spheres ensures that no aspect of a young person's well-being is overlooked in the conversation.

The chosen template for the goals, or how they are categorized, is not as important as the fact that goals are set. We cannot advise young people if we do not know where they want to go. The young person chooses the address, types it into the GPS, and controls the gas pedal and the steering wheel; in the passenger seat, we assist them in navigating the path and keeping an eye out for blind spots. Students will rise and fall to meet our expectations. If we expect something too far out of reach, they might quit before they even start. They want to save themselves from the embarrassment of failing. If we set an expectation too low for them, they will think, "Oh . . . that's what you think of me. Well, maybe that is what I am capable of."

As adults in the lives of young people, it is important that we set expectations for behavior, manners, and participation, but never should the setting of those standards give us the power to define someone else's success. Provide the space, time, and open discussion to establish where your expectations meet their goals. You should write out your expectations and ask your students to write their goals, then keep both documents somewhere visible. The posted goals serve as a reliable prompt for conversations when things are going well—and when things are not going so well. Revisiting the target regularly reminds the young person, and you, of the direction they are headed and highlights the motive and positive purpose of your relationship. These constant conversations about direction serve as layer after layer of trust being built over time.

Questions, Not Answers

As an awkward college kid, I was given invaluable advice by a mentor. When left in a room or on the sideline of a game with parents or people I didn't know, I should "just ask questions—everyone loves to talk about themselves." This one key piece of information has carried me through life, and saved me in countless situations. At plenty of cocktail parties, I've spent the entire evening asking questions and never revealing anything, only to find out later from an employer or friend that "so and so just adores you, they said you were lovely to talk to." While you might find this shocking, it isn't, if you think about it. The majority of people don't listen. While the other person is speaking, they fixate on what they are going to say next. When people run into someone who is curious, asks questions, and genuinely listens, they can't help but become enamored!

When I began using this tactic for social survival, I did not know it would become a crucial ingredient in my work with young people. Questions not only help you understand the other person's perspective, they help the other person understand themselves. Asking guiding questions of young people, rather than laying out all the answers, solidifies their own experience and thinking around the topic you are discussing.

It was spring sports tryout season, and students were stressing. Some students trained all year, waiting for "their season." Others searched for the right sport and activity, looking for a balance of competition and fun. And some longed for the activity that would require the least amount of their precious afternoon time.

Rachel, a first-year student who lived in my dorm, was eager to make the girls' varsity lacrosse team. She had determined that her sport was soccer. She easily made the varsity team and had an excellent season. She then, somewhat unexpectedly, made the varsity basketball team. Because of this, pressure was on to make the varsity lacrosse team. After she was cut, she ended up in tears on my front porch. I invited her in, made her a grilled cheese, and listened.

I desperately wanted to say to her, "But you have never played lacrosse, and you just think you're 'supposed to' make the team because you made the other teams, and you only want to be on the team because your best friend is on the team, and you just bought a lacrosse stick last week, and you will learn so much more on the JV team, and you can take a much needed breather from athletics and play for fun and for physical activity, but without the pressure of varsity . . . and . . . and . . . and . . ."

I knew, however, that if I spelled out for her all that I had learned in my life in athletics, she would roll her eyes and move on to another adult who might be able to help her. I can't make someone else see through my eyes, to take on my experiences as their own. Teaching isn't telling. Teaching is guiding. So, I took the question approach and asked: "Why was it important to you to make the team? What was special to you about your last two seasons—do you think the teams being varsity teams had anything to do with that? What are your future goals with athletics? What did the coach share with you when you were cut?"

Twenty minutes and about three grilled cheese sandwiches later, here is what she said: "I mean, I'm not even really sure how to play lacrosse, like all the rules and stuff. And to be honest, it isn't that fun—it's hard to catch and throw the ball. I could really use a season to focus more on my academics. And the coach said the JV team could really use my leadership skills. I think I was just expecting to make it, and I didn't, and so I was embarrassed. But I'm realizing all on my own, that it wasn't that important to me. I guess I didn't need you, after all."

As she left my house, I wondered if she really didn't need me, or if the trick was in leading from behind, allowing Rachel to believe she had come to her conclusions all on her own. A 2018 study out of Australia titled *The Role of Trusted Adults in Young People's Social and Economic Lives* confirms that "*talking not telling*" is the way to build the strongest trust with youth. Along with reporting that "trusted adults are linked to better physical and mental health among young people, fewer risky behaviors, and higher self-esteem," and that "trusted adults can have a beneficial impact on young people's education and employment," the researchers report that the best way for adults to become these trusted adults with such profound impact, is through their communication style: "The experience of *talking not telling* means that young people can seek the guidance they need for progressing through new formative life decisions, but this does not have to come at the expense of feeling like a child *or* of not getting the support they need." Though I had not read this study until years after my moment with Rachel, the JV lacrosse player, I knew when she left my house that day, as I stood holding my spatula, that the three keys to building strong relationships with adolescents were time, food, and questions.

Be Present and Do Something

I promised my ten-year-old son that I would take a day off from work so we could go to a water park. Wouldn't you know it, that morning I woke up to a crisis at school. I left him a note that I would be back soon, and we would do something awesome. "Soon" ended up being noon, and when I returned he was sitting at the kitchen table with his goggles, ready to go, but we no longer had enough time for the water park. Knowing how important it is to keep the promises you make, I was desperate to not break this one. Instead, I broke another parenting rule: I lied.

"Oh . . . you thought we were going to the big water park? I meant we were going to the 'mom water park.' It's what I used to do with my mom when I was a kid." (Lies)

"What's the mom water park?"

"You get in the car on a rainy day like today, and you drive to every playground you can find. You put your goggles on, get out, run to the playground, go down the slide, and run back to the car. It's so much fun!"

"Cool!"

I'll take cool. We got in the car, cranked up the music, and took off for our first playground. When we arrived, we parked (first spot in the lot, because nobody else goes to playgrounds on rainy days!), secured our goggles, and ran to our first slide. I'll admit—this was fun. Back to the car.

"You know who would love doing this with us? Dallas! Can we pick him up?"

"We sure can!"

The afternoon came to an end. We dropped Dallas off at home and laughed about our wild adventure. A year later, I again promised my son that I would take him to a water park. At bedtime, the night before we were supposed to go, he said, "Wait, are we going to the big water park or the mom water park?" Tempted to reveal that the mom water park was a scam, I stopped myself and, abiding by my questions not answers motto, asked, "Which do you prefer?"

"Well, I always love the big water park but the mom water park was my favorite. At the big water park you usually just sit in a chair and read or do e-mails and we just go on our own. But at the mom water park you had so much fun too."

"I'll make you a deal—if it rains tomorrow we will go to the mom water park, but if it doesn't then we will go to the big water park." And with that I put him to bed and said a little prayer for rain—the mom water park was way more economically friendly and fun, so can you blame me?! I also made a commitment to myself that if it didn't rain and we ended up at the big water park, I would put the e-mails away for the day.

My bedtime talk with my son reminded me of just how much our presence is desired in the lives of young people. They want to feel seen, heard, and valued. They want to play with us! Being present and doing something changes the relationship for the better. If the relationship can extend beyond the requirement, students feel a real investment and genuine care.

Going beyond just "doing something" and doing something that exposes your own vulnerability is the fertilizer that will enrich the relationship, making it grow further and faster. This tip is not just useful for relationships with young adults—it strengthens all our relationships. When I speak to audiences I often show them a video of me on a paddleboard for the first time. The clip starts with a beautiful setting on Lake Winnipesaukee in New Hampshire, framed by mountains in the background and subtle rolling waves. There I am, tense, standing on water, moving slowly. Then you hear my father-in-law shout, "Whatever you do, don't look down at the board." What do I do? I immediately look down at the board, then lose my balance and sprint off the front of the board, faceplanting in the water. It is a YouTuber's dream. I added a slow-motion effect and the song "Girl on Fire" to the video. Blown up on a big screen, it's priceless. The number of people who come up to me after a talk to say, "I can totally relate to your paddleboarding video, my first time paddleboarding I . . ." Apparently, faceplanting in water is a powerful connector. I think that if I showed a video of me paddleboarding successfully my first time out, nobody would approach me. There is connection in failure. There is connection in vulnerability. It is on us to actively choose not to just be the chauffeur or the chaperone on the trip to Six Flags, but to stand in line and ride the coasters.

When we allow young people to see us play, to see us try and succeed, or to see us try and fail courageously and gracefully, we give them permission to do the same. I have been taught how to play ultimate Frisbee and Quidditch, how to light a fire properly, how to tie strong knots, how to pack a hiking pack, how to Nordic ski, how to get up after falling on alpine skis, how to floss (the dance move, not the dental move), how to make a chicken pastry roll, and how to sing "We Are Family" while dancing choreographed moves in front of real people on a real stage, all by students. I would like to add that none of these things came naturally to me. As adults, we are supposed to have the answers, but what a gift we give when we turn the tables, fight back against the Supposed-To Syndrome we face, share our vulnerability and imperfections, and allow space for students to teach us. I would not have made it on a hike up Mount Moosilauke without the encouragement of one of my advisees. The chance to witness her way of motivating me gave me all the information I needed to motivate her when February of her senior year rolled around.

Most important, is to just be there, be present. Second, is to build trust through the layering of moments and memories, by doing something—anything!

Busy Hands = Busy Mouths

When you do something different, your conversations will be different from the regular small talk you repeat every day. Break the mold, and create space to learn, do, and say something new. Here are some activities that can get the conversation rolling with the young people in your care:

Go bowling	Watch a video	Play spike ball
Go rock climbing	Play minute-to-win-it	Make duct tape
Play a game of cards	Build trails	wallets
Bake something	Go for a walk	Build gingerbread
Write poetry	Defeather chickens	houses
Write thank-you	Roast a pig	Take a wood-
notes	Finish a puzzle	working class
Plan a school event	Do yoga	Learn a language
Make bracelets	Go grocery	Play Just Dance!
Read an article	shopping	

Almost anything that interests the young person you are talking with can work, so make suggestions for activities and ask what they'd like to do—you might be surprised by what you learn.

By being present and doing something, asking questions, hitting the mark with goal setting, and declaring our motive, we open the door to collaborating with young people rather than dictating to, or speaking at, them. These tactics for building trust apply to all our relationships. We do not need to have all the answers, and we certainly do not have to be the smartest person in the room. Rather than envisioning yourself sitting or standing in front of a young person, envision yourself sitting next to them. If they are working toward an achievement to please you or someone else, they are losing a valuable opportunity to target their own goals and set their own course. Allow space for young people to take ownership of their goals and choices, and to feel a personal connection to them. As an adult working with adolescents, this approach also relieves you of the expectation that you will have all the answers. It takes the pressure off and strengthens the impact you can have on those you mentor. Next, we will consider the approaches organizations can take to support you in this work and to create environments that foster meaningful and trusting adult–child relationships.

CHAPTER 5

Fostering Trusted Relationships at the Organizational Level

I was on the phone with a parent who was looking for guidance. His daughter, adopted from outside of the United States, is an incredible athlete; she is kind, helpful, and intelligent, but she struggles socially. He thought boarding school would be a great opportunity for her to learn to socialize by living with her classmates and teammates. Six months in, the experience was not what they had hoped for. She was isolated, lonely, and begging to come home. When I asked, "Has she found a trusted adult she can rely on?" his response was, "I just don't think this school is set up for that kind of thing."

If a school is not set up to build bridges between adults and students, if it does not foster an environment that creates more than a transactional relationship, then what is the purpose of school? David Brooks, in a *New York Times* opinion piece titled "Students Learn from People They Love," wrote that "what teachers really teach is themselves—their contagious passion for their subjects and students. . . . children learn from people they love, and that love in this context means willing the good of another, and offering active care for the whole person."

Youth-serving organizations must pursue their mission, write policies, train employees, and make many other important decisions that keep the focus on providing a safe space for young people to build trust with adults. Lisa Delpit, in her book *Other People's Children: Cultural Conflict in the Classroom*, says that "good teaching is not thought of in the same way in all communities." She goes on to note that "mainstream thinking holds that teaching begins with teachers' awareness of and ability to transfer knowledge." Unfortunately, the simple transfer of knowledge does not meet youth needs in a way that builds trust and creates connection. Delpit shares her insights—gleaned from conversations with teachers from communities of color and from her own personal experiences—that "many individuals believe teaching begins instead with the establishment of relationships between themselves and their students" and that good teaching requires that "the strongest relationship is between student and teacher, with content only being one aspect of their relationship."

With this thinking in mind, it is important for organizations to reflect on their current policies and approach, and assess whether relationship building is at the core of their program, traditions, and routines. Let's dive in and discuss actions that schools and organizations can take to create environments where adults are trained and encouraged to build trust and relationships with youth, including actions surrounding discipline and consequences, identity development, youth ownership, leadership, and representation.

Natural Consequences

When my son was six years old, we stopped by the post office on our way home from the bus stop. Normally, he would chat with the postmaster while I fiddled with the stubborn padlock on our box. On this day, he was fixated on the mailbox, crossing his fingers that he would receive mail.

"Any mail for me?"

"Nope."

Epic meltdown. "Why don't I ever get mail?" he screamed at the top of his lungs, launching the lollipop he'd just been given by the postmaster across the room.

"Do you ever send mail?" I snuck the question in between wails.

Reality check. Calmness. "Wait . . . do I need to send mail to get mail?"

"I can't guarantee that you will get mail if you send mail, but it will certainly help your chances."

He went home and wrote ten letters to ten family members across the continent. Within two weeks, he had received five letters back. He was satisfied with this 50 percent return rate, and I was satisfied that he was learning the concept of natural consequences. I can't guarantee that if you put kindness, love, respect, and fairness out into the world you will get it all back. But I can almost guarantee that if you don't, you won't. Natural consequences.

As important as it is for our schools and organizations to set clear rules and expectations for the sake of protecting the space and all members of the community, we should think carefully about how we can safely allow room for natural consequences to flow from young people's actions. In the educational world, there is consistent debate over philosophies such as punitive versus restorative consequences and practice. After-school meditation versus after-school detention offers one example.

In the book *Hacking School Discipline*, authors Nathan Maynard and Brad Weinstein report that "according to the Civil Rights Data Collection, of the 49 million students enrolled in public schools in 2011–2012, 3.5 million were suspended in-school, 3.45 million were suspended out-of-school, and 130,000 were expelled." The authors call on us as professionals to "realize that within every wrongdoing is a teachable moment. Further, we must take advantage of that moment rather than throwing it—and the student—out with the trash."

Educators are consistently searching for what will work to keep students' behavior in check. Rules and policies roll over from year to year and the administrative leaders who are expected to uphold the policies are not always the ones who wrote them. Policies can be outdated, meant for a different time and a different demographic of students. These outdated policies can inadvertently marginalize and punish certain populations, and cause a further divide between students based on factors such as gender, sexuality, race, ability, and socioeconomic status. Policies and rules need to be written and reviewed by teams that include students. The students are capable, aware, and arguably the most impacted by the written policies. Time and energy must be given to thinking through the rules, along with the response to violations of the rules. These teams must ask themselves:

- Where do we, and can we, allow for natural consequences?
- How can we make consequences logical to the infraction in our community?
- What restorative practices can we use to help heal those impacted?

Maynard and Weinstein go on to say, in a chapter titled "Throw Out the Rules," that "If students knew how to be successful independently, they would do it. But students need to be taught what to do, and that goes above and beyond teaching them what *not* to do. Teachers must expect success but also equip students with the tools necessary to reach our high expectations." Students must have choice, and consequences must make sense. I did not come to these thoughts on allowing space for natural consequences through research alone; rather, I was pushed to unlock my thinking about discipline the same way I am pushed in all of my thinking surrounding the role of trusted adults—in the trenches.

As a dorm parent in a small girls' dorm, I had six girls one year. One was a junior and five were sophomores. The junior, Jillian, had not been selected for a formal leadership position, but because she wanted to live in our dorm, I invited her to play a leadership role. She had not been formally chosen to be a part of the leadership team on campus because of some disciplinary trouble in her early high school years, and there was concern about her ability to make healthy choices. After getting to know her through these situations, however, I knew that deep down inside she had the makings of a caring, selfless leader. She needed to be given responsibility in order to rise up and show the world these characteristics. Lucky for me, she did. She took her role seriously, made smart decisions, and led by example—until she didn't. And then she learned the greatest leadership lesson of all time: hypocrites can't be effective leaders.

A colleague of mine came to me and said, "Hey, Jillian has a fish in her room, and is telling everyone, and then telling them not to tell Mrs. Raney. Isn't she your dorm leader?"

"Yup. Great . . ." We had a strict "no pets" policy, and this was a clear violation. I planned to talk to her about the fish that night. But that night, some other crisis took priority over the fish and I never got to talk to Jillian. Truly, I forgot about it. It wasn't until a couple of weeks later that the matter came to my attention again.

"Mrs. Raney!" Jillian was crying as she ran down the stairs of the dorm and into my kitchen.

"What's going on?"

In a frantic verbal rush she said, "I need to tell you something, but in order to tell you that thing, I would have to tell you this other thing, and I don't want to tell you the other thing, but I might have to tell you that thing so I can tell you the other thing."

I was lost. So I just started making more grilled cheese sandwiches.

"Take a deep breath, there's no hurry, think through what it is you want to share, and then I'm all ears."

"Well, it starts with a goldfish . . ."

Ah, yes, the forgotten fish.

"I know I'm not supposed to, but I have a fish. I get that it is against the rules, and I understand why, but I thought it wouldn't hurt anyone or anything for me to keep a goldfish in my desk drawer. Anyway, tonight, when I was trying to get everyone ready for study hall, one girl said, 'Why do we have to follow the rules? You have a fish,' and then later a girl tried to leave the dorm after hours to do laundry and when I stopped her she said, 'Why do I have to follow the rules? You don't,' and then again when I told a girl she needed to turn her light off she said, 'Oh really? Do you turn your light off? Because I know you love to break dorm rules.'"

Of course, I played dumb to any prior knowledge and naively asked, "You have a fish?"

"Yes, it was a weak moment, and it was stupid and not worth it. Now I know that if I break the rules there is no chance that I can uphold the rules. If I don't model it and lead by example, then there is no way to be a leader. And if I was those girls, and my dorm leader did this, I would treat her the same way. So I get it, I just have no idea what to do about it now."

Boom. Natural consequences. I wish I could say I had planned Jillian's comeuppance, that my skills as a trusted adult are so on point that I'd thought this all the way through and willed this moment to happen. I didn't. I simply forgot. And while Jillian was receiving an incredible real-life leadership lesson, I was seeing the benefits of just getting out of the way and allowing natural consequences to teach lessons instead of manufacturing discipline. My work as a trusted adult now came in the form of coaching Jillian on how to earn back the respect of her followers. And yes, my other role was to become the new adoptive mother of a goldfish named Gronk, who joined our family pet lineup of two golden doodles, Tuukka Rask and Larry Bird, and a hamster named Tom Brady.

If I had caught Jillian with a fish, taken it away, and metaphorically slapped her on the wrist, she would not have experienced the growth and development that came from working through the real-life consequences of her seemingly small choice. Buying a fish is not a life-altering decision, but choosing to consciously break a rule while in a position of responsibility is. When organizations call young people to the table, write and review policies as a team, agree on the appropriateness of natural, logical, and restorative consequences, they provide an opportunity for young people to feel ownership and investment. This practice also aids in providing students a full understanding of where the rules came from, why they are in place, who they are meant to protect, and how to work toward changing them. This transparency, coupled with the opportunity to contribute, builds valuable trust in the organization they are a part of, and, more importantly, trust in the adults leading it.

Self-Esteem Buckets

Within organizations, time tells us what is important. Take a look at the mission, then look at the schedule. Pay attention to the amount of time schools, camps, and sports teams allot to different categories. You will quickly learn the organization's real priority—time will tell a story about the reality and actual importance of the mission to that organization.

The other telling factor is what an organization chooses to celebrate in its people. The influence of community on individual identities is critical. Who we are surrounded by, what we are exposed to, and what we see being recognized and honored shapes our idea of success, which helps determine our choices and our future. At an impressionable age, I was lucky enough to be surrounded by adults who set me straight.

I moved from a small farming town in Ontario to a boarding school in Indiana with a similar-sized population. I arrived as a clueless fourteen-year-old with a sleeping bag and a pillow, as if I was going to a year-long summer camp. I had no idea what I was doing, except that I was there to play hockey.

My go-to introduction was, "Hi, I'm Brook. I'm a hockey player."

One soon-to-be trusted adult replied, "Oh yeah, what else are you?"

Dumbfounded, I just laughed. What an important question this stranger asked me. I had no idea how to answer it. For so long, I was the "girl hockey goalie." That was how I was known, it was an identity I embraced, and I didn't feel like I needed to be much else. Thanks to encouragement from incredible adults throughout my high school life, I participated and contributed in many different areas, but I still clung to my original identity for the majority of my self-worth and didn't let anything else define me.

In college, I finally took time to reflect on the "what else are you?" question, but only because I was forced to. Through these reflections, I have come to imagine self-esteem as a bunch of buckets. The buckets are lined up and represent the different parts that make up our identity as a whole. We are given a whole bunch of self-esteem pennies that represent pieces of our self-worth. For years, I chose, with encouragement through the messages I was receiving from my communities, to place all of my pennies in the ice hockey goalie bucket. Let me tell you, I had plenty of bad days as an ice hockey goalie.

One day, however, really stands out. I played for Colgate University, and we were predicted to lose by a "touchdown" to the University of New Hampshire. I was confused by this prediction, so my coach spelled it out for me: a touchdown is six points. They are predicting we will lose by six goals. Yikes! I had a friend on the other team, and I was determined to prove to her how great we were and spit in the face of the prediction. Well, not only did we lose by a touchdown, we lost by a touchdown *and* the extra point, 7–0. At the end of the game their fans threw a giant fish at me. Yes, you are hearing me correctly, a giant fish was launched over the glass and toward my net. I was unaware of this tradition, and when I caught sight of a fish flying toward me, I tried to dodge it in a panic. I fell flat on my face, giving the crowd exactly what they wanted—a flopping fish and a flopping loser of a goalie. It was a rough day, and the bottom of the only bucket holding my self-esteem pennies fell out. There was nothing left.

After that game, I questioned everything. Not only my hockey career, but my future, my passions, whether I deserved to live. It sounds ridiculous now, but based on a hockey game I questioned whether or not I should live. This is the danger of a single identity, of tying our self-worth fully to one part of who we are. I was fortunate enough to have a mentor who reminded me that I was more than a hockey player, and who had me sit down and write out my other valuable roles: babysitter, actor, friend, sister, daughter, Peer Leader, roommate. She made me write out my interests and passions too, explaining that they would someday, possibly, become a part of my identity as well. This exercise helped me sweep up my pennies and place them in multiple buckets. There would be more bad days as a hockey goalie, but this exercise helped me balance my self-worth and untie it from my performance in one area.

Organizations can help their young people build self-esteem by celebrating well-roundedness, encouraging a variety of accomplishments and talents. This does not mean everyone gets a trophy, or what child development specialist Betsy Brown Braun calls a "verbal doggie biscuit"—a "good job" for every action, even when it wasn't. And it also does not mean overdoing it and feeling the need to be a part of everything. Instead, the organization should create opportunities for all young people to showcase their interests and talents. The things young people see your organization spotlight in community meetings, online, in classes, in the locker room, and at graduation, become what they strive to do and be. Think carefully about what you want them to see. While maintaining your traditions for celebrating high honor roll, athletic hall of fame, and so on, make time to recognize and celebrate community service, students' essays or poems, the fastest Rubik's Cube whiz in your ranks, and your best beat boxer.

Whenever possible, encourage athletes to be artists, scientists to write for the literary magazine, and gym rats to volunteer at the local day care center. Let's fight back against the wave of specialization taking over our young people's self-esteem and allow them to explore, even as they excel in an area. There is no better time than middle school and high school, when we are surrounded by safe and encouraging adults, to seek what it is that we are most passionate about.

On the flip side, we must be careful not to promote the distribution of self-esteem pennies in too many buckets, spreading young people too thin. They do not need to be and try everything, just as they should not rely on being just one thing. Encouraging an appropriate amount of exploration balanced with the important life skills of commitment and time management will ground young people and help them avoid burnout through specialization or taking on too much.

By allowing students to safely try on different identities, we earn their trust, and by earning their trust we create the safest of places for them to explore their interests and try on different identities. It is a cyclical process that will keep itself going, once ignited. Take a walk around your physical space and read through your organization's social media feed; note how you have encouraged the distribution of self-esteem pennies into multiple buckets, and where you can do better, and in doing so create stronger connection and a deeper sense of trust with the youth you serve.

Creating Opportunities to Lead

So much of the work we do in building trust with young people comes from training and preparing and then getting out of the way. This is true for letting natural consequences hold sway and encouraging self-esteem buckets, and it is true of creating leadership opportunities as well. Strong organizations that are appropriately relying on their young people to lead operate from the following questions:

Adults ask: What are these young people capable of?
Young people ask: What will these adults let us do?

When adults and young people are encouraged to come together, to sit at the table and ask these questions out loud, they start the first conversation on the way to a student-led organization.

I founded the Girls' Leadership Camp (GLC) in 2011, and I ran the first week of camp with eleven girls. It was a brand-new concept, and there were no traditions to rely on or hold us back. I had the privilege and burden of starting from scratch. I could go on and on about all the wonderful benefits of the program (and there are many!), but what I want to share instead is a mistake I made.

A couple of years into the program we had eighty girls enrolled, and the girls asked if we could get together in the winter for a reunion, a reminder, and a midyear boost. I thought this was an excellent idea and promptly created a one-day conference for middle school girls that would do just that: provide a midyear reunion, remind them of what we worked on at camp, and give them a shot of encouragement to get through the winter.

I hired adult women to run workshops, and our high schoolers escorted the middle school participants from room to room. I thought it was great. As we continued to host this event, we had fewer and fewer high school girls interested in the program, even though the middle school numbers continued to grow. In the meantime, our organization planned a trip to Morocco for graduates of our GLC program. We took thirteen high school girls to Morocco for an exchange, and as the next step of their leadership development we trained these thirteen girls to facilitate workshops on confidence, self-esteem, public speaking, collaboration, and leadership with elementary and middle school girls in rural villages. In exchange, the Moroccan girls we worked with taught us Arabic. This experience was incredible, life changing at every level, for the young Moroccan girls, for the GLC high school girls, and for those of us who were orchestrating the trip behind the scenes.

It hit me after this travel experience that I had been doing the Midyear Boost all wrong. We were missing a huge opportunity for student leadership with the model we were using. The high school students were essentially Uber drivers, moving the younger girls from room to room, with no real investment in the program. The next winter, we rewrote the model and recruited hard, convincing eighteen girls that this would be an important and rewarding experience. We got together ahead of time and truly trained them. The day of the Boost arrived, sixty middle school girls registered, and the high school girls took charge. They were prepared and they delivered. The day was meaningful and magical—again, at every level: for the middle school girls, the high school girls, and those of us working behind the scenes.

One high schooler wrote: "I had an AMAZING time, and it felt amazing to not only get a winter boost myself, but also feel like I was helping others out. I thought the program was well thought out, I was trained properly, and I loved leading the girls. It made me feel a real sense of responsibility!!! My only wish is that the day was longer or we could do it more often!"

As leaders in organizations, we should center our thinking around providing training and space for student leadership. Modeling and celebrating all styles and types of leadership are important as well. The person with the microphone isn't the only leader. As a dean of students, I encouraged my faculty team to ask themselves, before signing up to give an announcement at an all-school meeting: "Can a student do what I am about to do?" Quite often, the answer is yes—it just takes a little more planning and a little more time. But the payoffs are huge. Student-advertised and student-led events are always far more successful and well attended than anything adults put on! And by leading successful events, young people are meeting many of the universal youth needs, such as belonging and membership, ability to contribute, independence, and mastery.

Investing in student leadership is key to success in an organization when all is well, but is also hugely beneficial in times of crisis or tragedy. When anonymous posting apps first hit the scene, schools nationwide struggled with what to do. Across the country, schools and other organizations were dealing with death threats, bomb threats, bullying, the leaking of private information—it was awful. I remember having lunch in the dining hall when a crying girl walked past me and whispered, so her peers could not see or hear her, "Mrs. Raney, check your phone." As I pulled out my phone, I felt all eyes turn to me. I had more than thirty e-mails about the horrible things being said about students and faculty on Yik Yak. The messages were a disgrace, and represented our community at its worst.

After I was up to speed, I sent out a message using the Yik Yak platform to let students know that I was disappointed and the negative messages needed to stop. The students then started pretending to be me and making statements like school was canceled for the rest of the day. Clearly, my tactic was not working. I did some quick research and learned that my next idea—bringing the community together for an emergency meeting—also seemed like a bad one. Other schools had tried this, and students wrote terrible things anonymously on Yik Yak about the principal while they were speaking, undermining the meeting and amping up the negative impact of the app.

Fortunately, our school had invested a ton of training and trust in our student leaders that fall, and they were up to the task. The next e-mail I received I had been only copied on, and it was from our all-school presidents, requesting that all student leaders meet in the auditorium. I was asked to just be an attendee of the meeting. I sat back and watched as they brainstormed ideas for addressing the situation. These high school leaders were committed to not letting hate and anonymous bullying disrupt the good work they had done to build a positive, happy, and healthy culture that year. Their idea was to kill the negativity with kindness. I gave them the nod, and off they went. The leaders had decided to overtake the app with kind messages about students and teachers, and to "like" all the nice messages, taking over the feed. It took hours, but they did it. And they felt proud. I was so proud of them. I trusted that their intentions were good, and my trust in them furthered their trust in me and in our organization as a whole.

Young people, like the rest of us, need to feel needed. We are our best selves when we take responsibility for something or someone.

Creating opportunities for young people to lead in classrooms, on sports fields, in the theater, and in other arenas might mean that you, as the adult, don't deliver the "perfect" result you had dreamed of, but the cost is well worth the growth of responsibility and independence in the young people in your care. One of the best ways to build trust is to give trust. Train the young people in your care, and let them know you trust them by getting out of the way. This will inevitably return the real result you are looking for: they will gain trust in you and your organization.

Look and Sound Like Me

Many organizations pride themselves on the diversity within their group of young people. This is magnificent. What an opportunity for all, to be surrounded by people of different nationalities, races, languages, socioeconomic backgrounds, talents, abilities, and other expressions. There are enormous benefits to living in and going to school in diverse communities and/or participating in activities with a diverse group.

The Century Foundation, a think tank that seeks to foster opportunity, reduce inequality, and promote security, compiled the educational research on this topic into an online article titled "The Benefits of Socioeconomic and Racially Integrated Schools and Classrooms." According to this article, research shows "diversity in the classroom can provide students with a range of cognitive and social benefits." Some of their examples included: higher average test scores; encouragement of critical thinking, problem solving, and creativity; reduction of bias; counterstereotyping; improved self-confidence; inclination to seek diverse settings later in life; and positive impacts on how people treat others who identify differently than they do. To cultivate an environment in which we seek, protect, and fully embrace diversity—and hold ourselves accountable when we fall short—we must recruit a staff that looks and sounds like our young people, and train all staff appropriately and regularly. This is an area where I have both succeeded and floundered.

The Girls' Leadership Camp I direct was pretty white: it is located in the middle of New Hampshire, and while we draw girls mainly from New England, we also found ourselves with attendees from New York, Texas, Maryland, Florida, Canada, and China. I (a white woman) was one of four founders of the camp, along with Shanterra McBride (a black woman), Christina Marin (a Latina woman), and Alexis Liston (a white woman). As the camp grew, we had many discussions about the diversity of both the campers and the staff. Most of the work to diversify fell on Shanterra, who is passionate about making the conversations inclusive and expanding the unique opportunity our camp represents to as many girls as possible. With the growth of the camp and the natural entrance of race into the dialogue about leadership, friendship, and body image, the conversations went to a whole new depth. Finally, our group had many more perspectives to share, and the benefits were invaluable.

What I, as director, had not fully considered was who we needed to hire to best embrace the demographic of girls we were choosing to serve. I had fallen into the trap of hiring people I knew, most of whom looked and sounded like me. They were qualified, and I believed would do an outstanding job, but it was the easy move, not what was best. What I had not yet come to fully understand, until the events below unfolded, was the importance of a staff that represented the youth we serve.

It was midweek of camp when a high school intern found me to tell me that a girl in her group had shared she was having suicidal thoughts and asked the high school intern to get her a knife. Fearful, but springing into action, the intern brought the matter to my attention. Immediately, I brought the girl to the nurse to be evaluated. When the white nurse and my white self sat down to talk to the black camper, a girl we had known for years, she told us that her grandmother had passed away and she was feeling really low. When I shared this information with Shanterra, hoping we could process together and make a decision with the nurse on next steps, Shanterra asked if she could talk to the camper. An hour later, here is what Shanterra told me and the nurse:

> Her grandmother died two years ago. This is not about the grandmother. She wasn't sure what else she wanted to share with the two of you. I sat with her for a little while, just sitting and breathing. She then, regretfully, shared that on the bus this morning she gave her counselor the middle finger behind her back. A few other girls saw it and looked at her with shocked faces. She was scared she was going to get in trouble for it, so she panicked and told her intern that she wanted to kill herself. She does not actually have thoughts of suicide.
>
> She is confused on who she is supposed to be at camp. She feels as though the white girls expect her to be a hard, tough, black girl, which is not actually how she would identify or what makes her most comfortable. At camp this summer she has created a hair salon called the "cell block," she has changed her way of speaking, and now she is giving the middle finger—all of this is not her true self. Her own behavior is confusing her. She is thirteen, in a diverse environment, trying to sort out who she wants to be and how that conflicts with who others want her to be.

I think my jaw hit the floor.

Given my identity as a heterosexual, cisgender, white female, I will not be the *best* trusted adult for all young people at all times. This is hard for me. Different young people at different times need to hear from, and be heard by, different adults. In some situations, more truth comes out when the adult they are talking with looks like them and sounds like them.

Organizations need to set themselves up for successful diverse environments by providing role models, through hiring and/or organizational partnerships, who look and sound like the young people in their care. In an interview with Perry Cohen, founder of The Venture Out Project, an organization that builds community for queer youth and adults via outdoor adventure, he shared that it is not impossible for a cisgender, heterosexual person to serve as a trusted adult for a queer student. (I use the word queer as an LGBTQ+ inclusive term used by the organization.) He told me:

> Connection can be hard to make if you can't see yourself in the adult you are working with, though it's not impossible. Organizations and schools should absolutely train the staff they have to be open, vulnerable, and to put themselves out there. And they also need to work tirelessly to staff their teams with a range of diverse individuals who represent the youth they serve if they want to attract, affirm, and retain diverse youth.
>
> As a young person growing up in the '80s and early '90s, I didn't have any openly LGBTQ+ adults in my life. I desperately wanted that connection but, since those adults probably didn't feel safe being out themselves, I found mentorship and guidance from adults who weren't necessarily queer themselves. I found that since I couldn't have queer adult role models, the adults I connected with most deeply were those who seemed to actually see me for who I was and who expressed recognition that they might be able to learn something from me. I believe that an open and excited cis/straight person showing their desire to build trust with a trans or queer person is affirming and powerful on both sides. I also believe our culture is being built by our youth, and it is crucial for us as adults to open up and learn from them.

When the leaders of organizations take the time and put forth the energy to really get to know their constituents, and make an effort to surround young people with the best adult role models possible, they prove to the young people in their care that they are worthy of their trust.

By allowing space for natural consequences and assessing disciplinary policies, encouraging a multifaceted identity and dispersing pennies in multiple self-esteem buckets, creating opportunities for students to lead and contribute, and recruiting staff who look and sound like your participants, your organization will foster an environment that encourages and supports relationships between young people and adults they can trust. The investment an organization makes in this approach to working with young people will improve all areas of your school, team, group, or camp, and, most importantly, place the focus on your greatest asset—your people.

Part II
Establishing Boundaries

CHAPTER 6

The Responsibility of a Trusted Adult

Trusted adults are the solution to many of life's problems for young people. We have established this, and we have confirmed ways you can identify yourself as a willing presence in the lives of young people, as well as specific ways to work toward building trust in your relationships. It isn't always easy, but it is always worth it.

The role of trusted adult carries with it a huge responsibility, and it should be taken with the utmost seriousness. Just as we train and grow in the specific traits and skills we use in our profession, we must train, grow, reflect, and always strive to do better and be better for the young people in our care.

"They saved my life" is a statement I hear often from those I interview about the trusted adults in their life. When I ask people to unpack that thought, I joke, "Did they take a bullet for you? Push you out of the way of a moving vehicle? Carry you out of a burning building? What could this person possibly have done for you to consider it 'saving your life'?"

One woman talked about a teacher: "He made me feel like a resourceful, capable, intelligent, curious friend to many—he saw good in me and celebrated it. In high school, it didn't feel like anyone else saw any of this, including my parents. He supported me unconditionally. He believed in me and convinced me that the struggles and problems I was facing (or creating for myself) didn't define me."

"How did you know you could trust him?"

"He was available, fair, and honest."

Another interviewee shared that her three aunts, who lived down the road from her, were absolutely her trusted adults: "They showed genuine interest in my well-being. They could see the future, but they only subtly tried to prepare me for it. They set the table for me but also stayed out of the way. They always pushed me to do more than I thought I was capable of. I am sure my mother was saying all the same things, but it just sounded more appealing coming from the aunts."

"How did you know you could trust them?"

"They trusted me. They included me in everything, and were always up for an adventure. It didn't matter if we were cleaning the yard, painting a fence, baking—they were always active, attentive, and engaged. Those conversations during window cleaning shaped my life."

All of these interviews bring the conversation back to the universal youth needs we talked about in chapter 1. Trusted adults make the young people around them feel safe, like they belong, and as though they have something to contribute to the group.

Embracing the Responsibility

Early in my career as an educator, the father of a young woman I was working with on a community service project wrote me an e-mail thanking me and letting me know that I was his daughter's role model. This pleased me and terrified me all at the same time.

I just thought we were working on a book drive together, and had not been intentionally building a relationship with this student. Looking back, I shake my head at my own thoughts and actions. "Not intentionally building a relationship?" What does that even mean? I had my mentees, my athletes, and my students—and this particular student, who I was working with on a special project, did not fit into any of my formal responsibility categories. She was outside my job description. So, as I actively tried to build relationships with all the other groups, I did not focus the same intentionality on this relationship. Then I got this e-mail, and it threw me. Now what? Should I act differently with her? If I know that I am her role model, does that change anything?

It did. Being reminded that the book drive was the avenue, not the destination, refocused my energy. On one of our early mornings lugging books from dorms to the library, I declared motive: "As an adult in your life, I hope you know it's my job to care about your health, happiness, safety, and success. I know we spend most of our time together sorting books, but if you ever need anything else, I want you to know I'm here for you." A subtle nod from her was all I got back. Years later, I received a letter from her sharing that, although she never needed anything else, knowing I was there for her gave her the confidence she needed to survive high school and continue seeking success.

We should be caring for all our youth in a fair and equal way, while individualizing our approach to meet their needs. Knowing you are a young person's "person" should feel like a weight on your shoulders, an extra responsibility, and an enormous privilege. As I have grown and experienced more types of students and more styles of relationships, I have finally built the knowledge and courage to feel confident stating the terms of the relationship and asking the young person what I can do for them in this role.

In my time as a dean of students, I sometimes found it difficult to build relationships with students, especially those who didn't always follow the rules, the ones who feared I was the "dean of mean" and could lay down the disciplinary hammer at any moment. I respected that certain students put their heads down to walk by me on the quad or didn't choose to swing by my office to chat. Being seen as unapproachable or scary was the most difficult challenge of that role for me, because my own assessment of my personality felt like a complete contradiction. My advisees, students in my dorm, and others relied on me and trusted me, but it took time and a strong commitment to develop that rapport.

A senior girl on campus, whom I knew but had not had any real interaction with over her four years of high school, unexpectedly signed up to volunteer for a school leadership event. She was incredible! She signed up without any friends, showed up early, brought a ton of energy, and totally shocked me. I thought I knew her—I had definitely put her in an identity box—and wasn't prepared for what I witnessed. Afterward, I received a note from her that included this line: "I have admired you from afar for a long time. I never knew how to start a conversation with you, or tell you how much I look up to you. Volunteering at the leadership day changed my life, and it gave me the courage to tell you that you are my role model."

After receiving this letter, I asked to meet with her. I began by thanking her.

"I cannot thank you enough for this letter, it means the world to me."

"You're welcome. I meant it."

"So it's your senior year, and you're just sharing this with me now?"

"Well, you seemed really busy, and you have so many students to take care of, I didn't want to be one more you had to worry about.

But last week's event was so amazing, and I just needed to tell you. And it's embarrassing to tell someone that you admire them."

"It's flattering! And it is a privilege to worry about you! Truly. I can't thank you enough for trusting me, and for your participation in the program. Now, I take the role of being an adult in your life seriously, and want you to know I am here to listen, help, and support. What is the best way to support you?"

Her eyes got wide. She had never been asked that question. It opened the door to a whole other conversation about her journey and her future dreams. In the end, she just wanted to know that she could stop by to check in and chat when she was free. This, of course, was a need I could meet—and wanted to meet. We didn't have many months left before her graduation but we have stayed in touch, and it has been a gift to be a small part of her story.

Things won't always go this smoothly. The responsibility of being a trusted adult often comes with more than book drives and office chats. When we enter into a young person's life as a trusted adult, we are agreeing to be there for all of it—the good, the bad, the difficult, and the sad. Remaining calm and consistent through the death of parents, the death of friends, suicidal thoughts, and college denials is tough at times. It is painful to watch another person, especially a young person, grapple with some of life's harshest realities. And although we cannot shield them from all of it, we can sit with them and face it together. Just being there, as I have heard again and again, and embracing the responsibility makes all the difference.

Avoiding the Responsibility

In every interaction an adult has with a young person, they have an opportunity to teach, encourage, and build up. This is true whether the interaction is daily, part of an ongoing relationship, or a one-off encounter. As an example, a server in a restaurant has an opportunity—whether they know it or not—to allow a child to feel seen, heard, and valued. Have you ever seen a server look to a parent to ask what the child wants to eat and drink? All the time, right? I have even seen this happen to a kid as old as sixteen, and the mother gladly told the server how her sixteen-year-old son preferred his burger cooked. Now, this is not always on the server—plenty of these interactions happen because the parent takes over the conversation and orders for the child. Either way, the child is left feeling incapable and without a voice. And if you are incapable of telling someone what food and drink you would like, then what *are* you capable of? I watch my son grapple with this daily. I witness him flex his independence and try and do things on his own, only to be shut down by adults who need my confirmation that he is capable before they will direct their attention to him.

You have heard plenty about him so far in this book, but what you might not know yet is that he is incredibly independent. I know this because we have encouraged him to advocate and speak for himself. How? By following advice outlined in Vicki Hoefle's *Duct Tape Parenting*. My favorite quote from Hoefle is quite simple: "the kids need us far less than we think they do." This reminder has helped me step out of the way and focus on training my son to eventually be a self-sufficient, functioning, and responsible adult. This includes, since he was very young, ordering his own food in restaurants, saving and paying for the toys and electronics he wants, and letting the barber know how he likes his hair cut. I could tell many stories about the times I've witnessed adults step back from the small ways they could have assisted in the growth and development of my son, but one day at the barbershop really stands out.

I had pulled him out of school for the afternoon for a doctor's appointment. We decided to cash in on the extra time together and run some errands, which included a much-needed haircut.

I do not care how my son gets his hair cut. I prefer it out of his eyes and trimmed above the ears, but his hair style is not something I want to go to battle over. This is what Hoefle teaches us: Is something so small and ever-changing worth a conflict with your child? My response is a definitive no. He can wear *his* hair any way *he* wants. Well, until he goes to the lake with long hair and his Grampy promptly gives him the zero summer cut—the natural consequences of being part of a military family! But that's *grand*parenting, not parenting.

As we arrived at the barber shop, I handed my son $20 in cash and told him to go get his haircut and meet me back in the car. I planned to use the time to make a phone call. Minutes after he left the car, he was back.

"I'm not allowed to go in the barber shop without an adult."

Though I was at first annoyed, I quickly came to my senses. As someone who speaks about adult–youth boundaries and healthy relationships, and during a difficult time in our country's history, with damaging adult-to-child abuses coming to light, I thought this a sensible move on the barber's part. Although I want my son to have independence and responsibilities such as getting and paying for his own haircut, I would oblige and go chaperone.

The walk across the street helped me overcome my impatience, and while I expected to be greeted by an older, small-town, veteran barber, I met the opposite. The absence of wedding and kids' pictures on the mirror and little decoration or memorabilia on the walls led me to believe he was new to town and probably not a parent. I let him know I was sorry to not have come in originally with my son, and I needed to make a phone call. He said that was fine and pointed me toward the single-chair waiting area.

He then proceeded to interrupt my call five times throughout the haircut to ask me questions that the young adult in his chair was fully capable of answering.

"Excuse me, how short do you want his sides?"

"It's up to him. He knows what he likes better than I do."

I knew in this moment that this barber was reading me all wrong.

"Excuse me, would it be okay if I went a little shorter on the top?"

"Again, he has been getting his own hair cut for years. Just ask him. I'm not up on the eighth-grade styles of today."

I tried to avoid his questions with jokes. I could read his assumptions: that my brushing off his questions meant that I didn't love my child. Despite my deflections, the questions directed at me continued.

"Excuse me, do you like it combed to the left or the right?"

"I have no preference."

My son spoke up, "Right."

What this barber couldn't see was that I allow my child the room to make his own decisions and voice his own opinion *because* I love my child.

Even though I am thoughtful about, and confident in, the way I parent, I still got enough pushback in this setting to make me feel guilty, as if speaking on behalf of my son, answering these questions for him and depriving him of his voice, equaled better parenting. I recognize that this barber's behavior is a reflection of the way he was treated as a young person, of the parenting he has witnessed, and of his professional training. I am certain that parents have been in his face making demands for their child's hair. The barber was trying to save himself a headache and please the person paying for the cut. I get it.

"That will be $15," the barber said to me, as I reached for the door handle.

Quietly, my son pulled the $20 bill from his pocket, thanked the barber for the haircut, and told him to keep the change.

Being on the parenting side of this story has reminded me to be intentional with all of my words and actions as the trusted adult, and especially as I train my camp staff. One of the most important lessons our camp staff learns on training day is that, during registration and drop-off, they should look the participant in the eyes, shake the participant's hand, and welcome them to the greatest adventure of their life! Then . . . and only then . . . they may greet the parent.

Every interaction with a young person is an opportunity to lean in and embrace the responsibility rather than stepping away and pulling the "I'm not the parent" card. Whether you are a server, a barber, a bus driver, a neighbor, or any other adult who may have an interaction with a young person, you own a part of the responsibility for growing the next generation. Be present for them, and look for moments to make them feel capable.

Exploiting the Responsibility

I prefer to tell stories about responsible trusted adults who have saved people's lives but we cannot continue without pausing to talk about people who have been placed in a position of trust and have taken advantage of young people, sometimes causing grievous harm. In recent years, survivors have come forward and journalists have brought to light abuse, scandal, and cover-ups occurring in organizations that pride themselves on caring for children.

Included in a 2019 BBC article are the results of a Church-commissioned report from 2004 stating that more than four thousand US Roman Catholic priests had faced sexual abuse allegations in the past fifty years, in cases involving more than ten thousand children, mostly boys.

Hitting very close to home for me as an educator, student, and believer in boarding schools, the *Boston Globe* in May of 2016 reported that among sixty-seven New England private schools, more than two hundred students over the past twenty-five years have accused private-school authorities of sexual abuse or sexual harassment; those accused included teachers, administrators, staff members, and (in one case) an admissions officer. The students' claims included rape, fondling, molestation, and oral sex. Even more concerning is the number of reports that prove the abuse often went unreported, and that when it was reported administrators "passed the trash" by terminating these abusers but writing positive recommendations so they could be employed at other schools.

In 2012, the *Los Angeles Times* released an interactive map revealing 1,900 files and 3,100 case summaries of abuse spanning from 1947 through 2005. These reports had been locked away for decades by the Boy Scouts of America. Viewing the map, it is striking and upsetting to see the vast number of abuse cases across the country through different troops. In response to this report, senior officials of the Boy Scouts wrote a letter that included the following sentence: "In certain cases, our response to these incidents and our efforts to protect youth were plainly insufficient, inappropriate and wrong."

Unfortunately, the list of abuses brought to light in the last decade continues. In 2012, Jerry Sandusky, former Penn State football coach, was sentenced to thirty to sixty years in prison after being found guilty of twenty-five felonies and twenty misdemeanors involving the sexual abuse of children. Larry Nassar, former USA Gymnastics medical coordinator, was finally sentenced to prison in 2018 after years of abuse claims from athletes. Beyond these headline news stories, which reveal numerous cases of child abuse and vast organizational cover-ups, additional instances of abuse and scandal continue at schools and organizations across the country.

You may be reading this and thinking, there is no way I could do anything like what these criminals have done to young people. I would hope not. But I share these traumatic events here because they are an unfortunate reality, and the potential for grooming and abuse is something we must all remain hyperaware of. Experienced education lawyer and Title IX investigator Kai McGintee told me in an interview:

> When we label sexual interactions between children and adults as "abuse," we conjure an image that is not aligned with how these interactions actually take place. Often, and particularly with those that involve adults in positions of trust and authority, these interactions and relationships do not appear "abusive" at all. There is no force, no physical coercion, no aggression used to facilitate the adult's sexual interaction with the child. As a result, when we do not see these signs of abuse, it is hard to identify that the "sexual abuse" could be occurring within the adult–child relationship. It is particularly hard to believe that it could be occurring in relationships that appear to be built on trust, care, support, and closeness. Nonetheless, that is precisely the foundation upon which they are built.
>
> Long before "sexual abuse" occurs in a relationship, there are numerous small and possibly innocent-appearing interactions in which boundaries are crossed and lines are blurred. These boundary crossings and blurred lines, not abusive behavior, are how grooming begins. Whether intended or not, they can also lead to significant harm to the child whether that be in the form of emotional, psychological, or sexual harm.
>
> This is not to say that every close and trusting adult–child relationship leads to sexual harm. Not at all. Rather, when trusting, caring, and supportive adults maintain healthy boundaries with children, they cause no harm and instead emotionally, psychologically, and intellectually lift up the child. This, to me, is why we need to understand the damage that broken adult boundaries afflict on

children as well as the potential and power that healthy adult boundaries bolster in children.

McGintee reminds us in this interview that most abuse is circumstantial rather than calculated, that teachers, priests, doctors, and others do not necessarily set out to be predators but instead blur boundary after boundary, and make their way to a place where abuse can easily occur without looking much like abuse to the outside world. These cautionary words also reveal that there is plenty more we can do, as protectors of youth, to educate adults, inform young people, and better prepare our organizations to fulfill their number-one job of keeping children safe.

Dr. Thomas G. Plante, in a *Psychology Today* article, "Separating Facts about Clergy Abuse from Fiction," wrote about preventing and responding to child abuse:

> Keeping children safe from abuse should be everyone's top priority. Tragically, data suggests that whenever men have access to and power over children and teens, clerics or not, a certain small percentage of them will violate that trust and sexually abuse these minors under their supervision. This is true for Catholic and non-Catholic clerics as well as lay teachers, coaches, tutors, choir directors, scout leaders, and so forth. The best way to deal with this reality is to develop evidence based best practices that create environments where children are safe and where you carefully screen for those who wish to work with young people. Doing this has been very successful with many organizations during the past decade or so including with the Catholic Church, the Boy Scouts, Boys and Girls Club of America, US Olympic Committee, public and private schools, and so forth (and all of these organizations have consulted with each other to ensure that best practices are known and followed).

Following the advice of Dr. Plante, later in the book we will tackle the importance of holding colleagues accountable and understanding mandated reporting responsibilities as well as other best practices for creating safe environments for youth. Before we get there, I would like to offer two other examples that, though they pale in comparison to the crimes above, blur lines and confuse relationships in similar ways.

A teacher I met recently said to me, "I didn't have a good trusted adult, but I can tell you about a bad one." Here is what she wrote:

> I had a Spanish teacher in 7th grade, and she was everything to me. I totally admired her. She wore cool clothes. Had a cool way of interacting with us. And often let us off the hook and didn't expect much of us. When I think back, I don't remember learning any Spanish that year.
>
> I used to come in to school early to help her with projects, and stay late after school—she would drive me home. When we started spending more time together, she started opening up and telling me about her life. It was probably more than I could really comprehend in 7th grade. She had recently been divorced, found out she couldn't have children naturally, she had an abusive father, and she was struggling with an eating disorder. I didn't even know what an eating disorder was, but I knew I wanted one. I wanted to relate to her. I started writing her letters describing my eating disorder (that wasn't real), and she always wrote back. I also wrote to her with lies about how my parents were treating me, and that my dad was abusive. She bought it. She baited it. She celebrated it. She rewarded it.
>
> The situation grew until I really was starving myself. Inadvertently (I think), she was teaching me how to have an eating disorder, how to get away with it, and why I should have one. What a confusing time as a 7th grader. It escalated until my parents stepped in and spoke with the principal. I don't know the details of what occurred, but I know I was mad that I could no longer go to school early or stay late,

and that the letters had to stop. As an educator, looking back now, I just can't imagine speaking to my students the way she spoke to me, and blurring the lines like that was so hard to understand. It really put a strain on my relationship with my parents. She was clearly hurting and not in a good place herself. Self-care needs to be a part of your book, Brook! We cannot take care of others if we can't take care of ourselves.

Was this abuse? No. But it is definitely an example of an educator who does not understand the responsibility of her role. It is an example of a boundary blurred so badly that an adult woman is still processing her seventh-grade experience. The teacher was certainly trying to connect, but in all the wrong ways. Just being there for young people, as I have stated in other chapters, is a baseline for this work. But if you are being there to serve your own needs and not the needs of your students, then you are doing more damage than good. We will dive further into this in the next chapter. For now, I'd like to share with you my own personal experience with a confusing and blurred boundary.

When I was in eleventh grade, my friend wanted to get a tattoo. I was intrigued but not interested for myself. I absolutely wanted to go with her, but I had no desire to have anything permanently inked on my body. Her parents said no, they would not take her to get it, and she was not allowed to get one. We were in the rebellious phase common among seventeen-year-olds, and she was not going to let this one go. She asked the assistant coach of our hockey team if she would take us. Immediately, the coach said yes, and seemed overly excited. She was a young, single woman living in a small town, with not much else going on.

After practice one night, the assistant coach took the two of us to a tattoo parlor about twenty miles away. She signed as our guardian and even lent us money. My friend got her tattoo and, although I went with no intention to do anything, I walked out with a tongue ring. Yes, in 2002, at seventeen, under the supervision— and with the encouragement—of an adult hired to coach and care for me, I got my tongue pierced. It did not last long, and there is a whole other story to write about my father's reaction, the hockey game I missed due to infection, and the class I got kicked out of because of the stupid tongue ring. I bring this up now because, as a coach, I cannot imagine taking a minor, a player whose parents trust me, to a tattoo parlor! This coach thought she was gaining our love and admiration, and maybe she did for a moment, but within months—for this reason and a variety of others—we players lost all respect for her.

Regardless of the weight of the boundary infraction—from tattoo parlors and oversharing to emotional and sexual abuse, three factors are common to the organizations where such boundary-crossing takes place:

1. **Absent and/or ineffective leadership.** If the safety of children is not a number-one priority for the leadership of an organization, then it is unlikely to be a priority for the team of trusted adults under their direction.

2. **Lack of colleague-to-colleague accountability.** Breaking the silence and preventing abuse begins with colleagues seeing something, saying something, and holding one another accountable.

3. **Nonexistent or infrequent training on personal and professional boundaries.** Training on boundaries should be as regular and as important as technology training, fire drills, and CPR certifications.

In a 2017 article titled "My Turn: The Path to Preventing Teacher Sexual Abuse" in the *Concord Monitor*, David Finkelhor, the director of the Crimes against Children Research Center, writes that "it is a good sign that the spotlight is now on schools and teachers. A new page in youth protection is being written." I appreciate his hopeful tone, and I, too, believe that we can and will, as adults invested in the next generation, do better to protect young people. The keys, Finkelhor says, to youth-serving organizations fully embracing the responsibility of being trusted adults, beyond good hiring practices (reference and background checks) are: managing offenses (the age of quiet terminations is over), explicit boundary training, encouragement and expectations to hold one another accountable, and self-management tools that help adults balance personal life with professional life. In the following chapters, we will tackle exactly this, and discuss why boundary training is important, beyond the primary focus on the safety of children and prevention of abuse, as well as outline specific strategies for establishing these necessary clear and healthy boundaries.

CHAPTER 7

Why Boundaries? Why Now?

A young faculty member I worked with recently told me that she "really screwed up" in her first job at a school. After college, which she completed in three years, she had returned to the high school she graduated from to teach. Because of her quick return, there were still students at the school who knew her from her time as a student.

Initially, this young teacher thought her personal ties were a great way in and perfect for connecting with students, but she quickly learned that her familiarity with students made it difficult to establish her status as a professional. She spent two years battling to be seen as a responsible adult by the students and her colleagues (her former teachers). Eventually, she gave up and, feeling defeated, applied to other schools. She moved to a new school, where her only boundary training consisted of her boss's advice: "Just be mean until Halloween, and they will respect you." She asked me honestly, "Mean 'til Halloween? There must be more advice out there on establishing healthy boundaries, right?"

There is, but there is also resistance to spending as much time training educators and others who work with kids for their roles as trusted adults as we do preparing them in other aspects of policy and practice. Trust and appropriate boundaries form the basis and the foundation for the work we do, and if these are missing, there will be little education and growth to be found. I am not a lawyer, a social worker, or a health professional, but my wealth of experience as an educator, dean of students, and camp director, together with professional conferences and trainings on the topic of boundary setting, have given me a sincere appreciation for its critical importance in our work. I sought this type of training, but wish it had been more accessible to me as a young educator, and that it had been offered as a regular part of my training rather than me having to seek it out. I firmly believe that if we spend more time training adults on building and maintaining clear and healthy boundaries with young people, we can prevent abuse and grow future adults who understand and are able to establish healthy boundaries in their relationships.

What Are Boundaries?

Think of a boundary as a declaration of expectations and an agreed-upon way to work together. Shifting our thinking about boundaries away from the idea that they concern primarily the keeping in or keeping out of people or objects makes establishing boundaries far easier and less scary. In any relationship, we can either take control and set our expectations surrounding physical touch, intellectual exchange, emotional vulnerability, material sharing, and time, or we can leave these boundaries to be sorted out as questions arise, which can lead to confusion and disagreement. People with clear boundaries are not mean people, they are smart people. Different people have different boundaries, and those may change based on context, culture, time, and type of relationship.

In an online interview, Brené Brown, author of *Daring Greatly* and other must-reads, says, "One of the most shocking findings of my work was the idea that the most compassionate people I have interviewed over the last thirteen years were also the most boundaried." She explains that people allow things to happen and then are resentful, rather than setting boundaries and expectations up front. I find that teachers, coaches, camp counselors, and other adults do a great job outlining classroom norms, team expectations, and group rules but do little on a one-on-one basis to clearly define boundaries in their individual relationship with the student.

Brown challenges us to ask the "BIG" question: What **boundaries** need to be in place for me to stay in my **integrity** and make the most **generous** assumptions about you? We struggle to set boundaries because we have conditioned ourselves to believe that boundaries are selfish. Brown makes the case that clear and healthy boundaries allow us to be our most selfless, caring, and giving selves.

What Do Boundaries Look Like?

As a concept, boundaries can seem simple but in reality they are complex, can change in different circumstances and with different people, and need constant attention. Every action, big or small, sends a message to those around us about our personal and professional boundaries. So, what do healthy boundaried people look like? Let's take a look at specific behaviors that can inform us about the boundaries of others and, most importantly, identify our own habits when it comes to building boundaries.

Too Loose: Trusts everyone, speaks intimately at first meeting, does not recognize poor boundary setting in others, acts in opposition of personal values for purpose of pleasing others, inserts self into problems of others, accepting of abuse or disrespect, self-worth comes from others' opinions

Too Rigid: Trusts no one, avoids close relationships, does not ask for help, protective of personal information, seems detached, avoids vulnerability for fear of rejection, black and white thinking patterns

Just Right: Allows trust with others to develop over time through a layered approach, values own opinions, keeps focus on growth and development, notices when someone else lacks healthy boundaries, clearly communicates wants and needs, accepts when other's say no, shares appropriately personal information based on trust built in a relationship, self-worth comes from within

Looking more closely at boundaries, which can be either too loose, too rigid, or just right, let's think back to stories you have heard so far in this book: the barber, the Spanish teacher, the drum teacher, the aunts, and Mrs. O'Neill.

Recall the story of my teenage son's experience getting his hair cut and not having the chance to say a word or express an opinion. Whatever the barber's personal history, it led him to a place of rigid boundaries with his customers, specifically young people. This is not wrong or bad, but he chose to make his interaction transactional instead of taking an opportunity to make the most of a moment with a young person. I was not seeking a life-changing experience for my son in the barbershop, but I do look for opportunities for him to feel seen, heard, and valued, and to practice his independence. When rigid boundaries are in place, there is little room for anything more than the delivery of a service (teach a class, run an activity, coach a practice, provide a haircut). Following the transaction, everyone goes in their separate directions. Nothing earth-shattering happens either way—positive or negative, but a moment with a young person was missed.

On the flip side, we heard a story of the Spanish teacher who revealed personal information about an eating disorder, divorce, pregnancy, and an abusive father to her seventh-grade student. This is a perfect example of oversharing personal information, and boundaries that are far too loose. While the boundary descriptions mainly explain the ways adults interact with one another, there is some crossover to relationships with young people; I would add to the "Too Loose" description for adult-to-young person boundary traits that the adult relies on the affection and admiration of the young people in their care and works to build this admiration by divulging information that is not appropriate or necessary for a young person to know. When others' opinions matter more to the adult than their own opinion of themselves, they work in the wrong areas to build relationships with youth, who don't yet have a foundation for setting their own solid boundaries.

In the stories of my son's drum teacher and his wise words, the aunts down the street with their window-washing conversations, and Mrs. O'Neill, the sage mountain climber, we hear about adults sharing just enough. We sense that there may have been much more to their stories, but the adults knew exactly how much to share in order to connect with the young person, yet not burden them emotionally. These adults understood how to teach a lesson through an activity they were participating in rather than through personal stories of heroic triumph or painful tragedy. And they knew how to communicate carefully and thoughtfully in expressing values and opinions.

Boundaries are established criteria for how we will work together, both one on one and in groups. Rather than regarding these limits as scary or harsh, we should consider them an opportunity for defining how we can work together in the healthiest and most positive way.

Why Should We Take the Time?

Now that we have established what boundaries are and what they look like, let's talk about why we need to train our adult teams on their importance. There are so many policies, best practices, and day-to-day logistics we have to convey to our team that training on boundaries often falls to the bottom of the list. Here are four reasons it should stay at the top!

1. **Protection and safety.** The number-one result of clear and healthy boundaries is the safety and security of children—and this is obviously of paramount importance. I do not want to lose sight, however, of *your* safety and security. If you are being asked by a supervisor or an organization to do something that is outside your established professional boundaries, you must protect yourself as well. The number of times I have heard stories from people whose superior asked them to do something outside their job description, beyond the scope of their training, or that might be neglectful or even illegal is beyond belief. Protect yourself, and let your personal and professional boundaries be known. If you lead an organization, the safety and longevity of your organization also rely on establishing boundaries. If you have people working for you who have not been trained by you on establishing clear boundaries, and then an issue of blurring lines (or worse) arises, you are putting your organization and all of the people in its care at risk.

2. **Sustainability.** Self-care is critical to the longevity and significance of your work with youth. I have witnessed firsthand a new educator burn himself out in one year because he attempted to be all things to all people. You are not a superhero. Although superheroes and educators possess similar qualities, there are limits to your service, your impact, and your time.

We hear over and over again the example of the airplane oxygen mask. I reiterate it here because I sometimes need the reminder too. If we do not follow the flight attendant's advice that, in an emergency, we put the oxygen mask on our own face before assisting others, we impair our ability to help others. If we are not operating with good sleep, wholesome food, plenty of exercise, reliance on a positive community, and inspiration for mind, body, and spirit, then we are not as able to educate, be relied upon, or sustain healthy boundaries. When you care for yourself, you will feel stronger about protecting your reputation, your vision, and your personal and professional impact. Self-care and boundaries lead to a sustainable and gratifying career.

3. **Modeling.** Good relationships require good boundaries. Whether with siblings, spouse, friends, or colleagues, our interactions with other humans are shaped by what we allow and what we disallow. The young people we work with may grow up in homes with too loose, too rigid, or rightfully healthy boundaries, and their history with boundaries, unbeknownst to them, will shape their interactions with you. You will be only one piece—though an influential one—in their development of their own boundaries. As they get to know you and your way of setting expectations for how you treat others and are willing to be treated, what do you want them to see? The boundaries you establish with the young people in your care will influence what they emulate in their adolescent and adult relationships. This is an enormous responsibility. We teach our students, athletes, and campers so many skills, but how often do we teach them the concept of relational boundaries? Formal teaching in this area is rare, so what young people learn comes from what they see. And what they see is you.

4. **The line.** A boundaryless world is terrifying for young people. In my house growing up, I knew where the line was, and knowing that gave me the room to practice getting really close to the line, dancing on the line, tiptoeing over the line—and understanding when I had crossed the line. By establishing household expectations and family values, my parents gave me a wide open field on which I could test my independence without falling off into an abyss.

I remember smoking cigarettes for the first time and being so terrified my parents would smell it on my breath that I ate a whole tube of toothpaste. Growing brain, growing pains. The toothpaste made me sick, and between moments heaving over the toilet my guilt made me confess. I knew the boundary and I knew the consequences. The friend who tried the cigarettes with me had a different set of rules, different family values, and a relatively boundaryless world to explore. When we were young, she never got caught, never regretted her decisions, and never questioned whether anyone would be upset or disappointed in her—and now, she is in and out of prison. Her boundaries were legal, not lines drawn by trusted adults, and like most adolescents she found the line, danced on it, tiptoed over it, and ultimately got lost in the abyss. Boundaries are necessary guidelines, an establishment of priorities and values.

How Do We Create Boundaries?

We have established what boundaries are and why we need to focus time and attention on training adults in setting boundaries. Now, how do we do it?

As excited as I was to tackle the idea of boundaries with my team, whether at camp or at school, I was always met with resistance. One adult would speak up and say, "We are all experienced educators—we know how to not abuse kids." My response assured my teams that I was not accusing them of being abusers and that the world was constantly changing, teens were constantly changing, and we needed to keep up. "It's just like CPR," I would tell them. "Even health professionals who went to med school have to update their CPR certifications. There is no reason we should not continue practicing our skills in this area and discussing how we might handle specific situations. Boundaries are about much more than child abuse."

The best way to train in boundary setting is to practice, just as with anything else we want to get better at. Below are five scenarios I use to help teams sort through and discuss appropriate boundaries and how to behave when a boundary is crossed. Following the scenarios is a list of considerations you can use to evaluate how you would handle the situations.

Scenario 1

You have a new student assigned to you as a mentee. Things have been going well for this student throughout their first few weeks at school. You are impressed with this student's work ethic and instant engagement in the community. Over fall break, this student e-mails you because their travel plans changed and they need a ride from the bus station. You e-mail back and let the student know that you are available and happy to pick them up. You provide the student with your cell phone number so they can text you when they are thirty minutes away. Providing your mentees with your cell phone number has never been an issue in the past. Weeks later, you start receiving numerous texts from this student at all times of day and night. Some of the content is harmless and silly and makes you laugh, but much of it is full of complaints about peers, food, grades, teachers, and parents.

Scenario 2

You are meeting with a student to discuss their recent midterm comments. The conversation goes like this:

> Teacher: "How are you feeling about your comments?"
> Student: "Fine."
> Teacher: "Have you thought about any goals for improvement?"
> Student: "Not really."

Teacher: "Well, your history teacher mentioned that it might be a good idea to go to office hours more often, especially before quizzes. Can we make that a goal?"

Student: "Won't make a difference."

Teacher: "Why not?"

Student: "She hates me."

Teacher: "That is not true."

Student: "Yes it is. Mrs. X told me."

Teacher: "What do you mean?"

Student: "A couple weeks ago, Mrs. X was on duty in my dorm and we were hanging out. I was telling her how I was struggling in history class and she asked who my teacher was. When I told her she said, 'Oh yeah . . . I heard her talking about you in the faculty meeting. She said you are lazy and you're not living up to your potential or something like that.' So there . . . she hates me. It's confirmed."

Scenario 3

You are a new assistant coach of a varsity team, and you really love the head coach you work with. A few weeks in, you are winning, and from the outside it looks like a great season, but you have noticed a pretty negative locker-room culture. The team often uses the time in the locker room to make fun of others on campus, and to say vulgar and inappropriate things. You have overheard a couple of statements that made you uncomfortable, but you believe that the head coach heard them too, and you don't want to step on toes. You can't tell if the coach is oblivious or is purposefully ignoring the behavior. The behavior continues, until one day in the hallway you hear one of the team members make a horrific statement about another student you know well. You step in and say, "That's enough. You have completely crossed a line, and I don't want to hear you speaking like that anymore." You are met with a response from the captain, in front of most of the team, who says, "Why? Coach doesn't care."

Scenario 4

In a homeroom meeting, one of your students complains that they need to leave early because they have a huge assignment for Mr. X's class due the next day. Another student perks up and says, "Why don't you ask for an extension? I did, and my project isn't due until Thursday." The other student can't believe it, and claims that they did ask for an extension and were denied. You try to insert yourself to explain that there can be different scenarios and circumstances, and you are sure Mr. X has good reason for his decisions. The student who received the extension then says, "Or it could be that I'm his favorite." There is a cockiness in the voice of this student that leaves you annoyed with their behavior. You keep this student after class to talk about what they said.

Teacher: "I don't think the others in the group appreciated when you made the comment about being Mr. X's favorite. Especially when one of them is stressed about a project they have due for him tomorrow."
Student: "Well, it's true."
Teacher: "Why do you say that?"
Student: "He told me . . . look at this e-mail."

The e-mail from Mr. X, granting the extension, includes a sentence that reads: "Every teacher has a favorite and you are mine."

Scenario 5

You are in your first year of teaching, and scored a job at a well-established school. You moved into your classroom, got your computer, and went through a grueling new faculty orientation.

A ton of new information came at you at once, but you are confident and ready to begin. After the first few days of classes, you notice that your Instagram and Snapchat are flooded with requests from your students to follow you. You are excited because you take this as a sign that they like and respect you.

A few months later, at a faculty meeting, there is a reminder that faculty and students are not to be connected through social media. You consider removing the students from your contacts but eventually decide that there is no harm. Shortly after this, there is an incident of vandalism on campus: the gym is broken into and spray painted. This is a big issue on campus, and all faculty members are asked to bring forward any information they have. While scrolling through your snap stories, you notice a video on one of your students' stories that shows the student performing the vandalism. You now know who the culprit is but you are concerned because disclosing the information would reveal that you disregarded faculty policy.

What Would You Do?

After reviewing Scenarios 1–5, consider what would happen if these scenarios occurred within your organization. What would you do? As a team of trusted adults, work through the following question for each scenario. Imagine yourselves taking on the role of the adult in the situation, as well as considering the perspective of the parents, the child, and the school administrators.

1. What possible issues/concerns might this scenario raise?
2. How could this situation result in a violation of the law or school policies?

3. In this situation, what are some potential negative consequences for the teacher, the students, and the school community?
4. What responses/actions should be taken at this point in the scenario?
5. What proactive measures might be considered to prevent this sort of occurrence in the future?

The first time I presented these scenarios in a training session, a participant questioned their usefulness, with the attitude that "none of this would happen here." I had to burst this person's beautiful bubble and explain that, unfortunately, all of these situations had happened at schools just like ours; although they had not happened at our school, these were real scenarios shared by real school administrators. Youth-serving organizations consistently deal with big and small violations of boundaries, many of which, I argue, could be prevented through training and practice. Often, these issues are private and confidential, and cannot be shared with the greater team of adults. Just because you don't hear about them, do not assume they are not happening; instead, train to prevent them.

Now that we have established what boundaries are, why it is important we take the time to discuss them and practice boundary setting, and potential scenarios you can work through with your team, we will shift to actions that trusted adults can take to establish clear and healthy boundaries with the young people in their care.

CHAPTER 8

Maintaining Boundaries: Protecting Youth and You

I started chapter 4, "Building Trust and Making the Most of the Moments," by sharing that most adults answer "they were just there for me" when asked why, as young people, they trusted certain adults. The second most common answer is, "They made me feel safe and like I belonged." People trust those who make them feel safe. Boundaries and a clear outline of expectations create a feeling of safety, and develop a space where young people feel a sense of belonging and acceptance for who they are. Quite simply, there is no true trust if there are no boundaries.

Below, we will explore what to share with young people and how to share it, the appropriateness of affection, ways to resolve conflict, and the tried-and-true "shoulder test." All of these tips and reminders are important to practice when taking a layered approach to establishing boundaries and building trust, day after day, moment after moment.

Tone and Intention

I was teaching public speaking, and in the class I had students from six different countries: the United States, Spain, China, Korea, Mexico, and Russia. What a fascinating experience it was. The class was taught in English, and all of the students had excellent reading comprehension. Most had excellent oral comprehension as well. Speaking, however, posed challenges for some. I worked hard to understand what the English language learners were trying to communicate, but sometimes I fell short. Typically, they would deliver their speech once in English while I followed their script, and they would then recite the speech again in their preferred language so I could see their progress on emoting, body language, eye contact, enthusiasm, and so on. I was in awe of the way they came alive in their own language, and what a different person they appeared when they were more relaxed and not struggling with the words. Tone and intention through oral and physical communication make an enormous difference with the message we receive and how we receive it.

I always attempted to have students deliver their speeches to another audience, a group other than me and their classmates, that would find meaning in what the student was sharing. Once, Alejandro, a student from Ibiza, Spain, asked if he could write a speech about his home and share it with local students who were taking Spanish. I looked for a school to make this possible, and found a local eighth-grade Spanish teacher who was interested in hosting us. I drove Alejandro to the school later that month, he set up his PowerPoint, and the teacher nodded to begin.

"First, I want to tell you about the best part of Ibiza: the b*tches."

The eighth-grade students' heads turned to the teacher, the teacher's head turned to me, and I turned red.

"In Ibiza there are many big b*tches. Some are dirty b*tches. Some are clean b*tches. But everywhere you look in Ibiza, you will see a b*tch. Let me show you."

He clicked for the next slide, and a beautiful picture of a *beach* popped up on the screen. Everyone in the room silently let out a breath and chuckled to themselves. I'm not sure how much the students in that classroom learned about Ibiza that day, but they certainly got a lesson on the importance of pronunciation, tone, and intention. What we say is not always what others hear. Although the above story is a cute one about the mishaps that can occur through pronunciation and language, it reminds us of how important it is to consider, practice, and talk through our intended message before we deliver.

Have you ever told a joke or made a well-intended humorous comment that didn't land well? I have! When you see the reception of your joke and immediately know it was taken differently than you intended, you may feel devastated. Although we cannot pull back and swallow the words, our job instead is to recognize how our behaviors and words impacted others, apologize, and move forward with the best intentions to do better and grow. One important piece of advice a colleague shared with me once was, "Intention is invisible." And this advice was given to him before text messages and e-mails even existed!

Intention in our interactions with other people (online and in real life) is not visible to them. Our words can cause unintentional hurt and shame to others, but explaining that they were not intended in the way they were received will not change the feelings they elicit in others. It is imperative that we pay close attention to the words we choose and the way we deliver them, especially with the young people we serve, who are reading between every line and sniffing out every discrepancy and bit of hypocrisy. We must be clear about our meaning and our motives, and our tone must match what we are communicating. If you are not sure your message is getting through as intended, ask the young person to repeat back what they understand you to be saying or what they have taken from the conversation.

Countless times, as a dean of students, I had situations land in my office that were less school violation, and more massive miscommunication. One situation that fits this description included a car trunk, a local deli, and an adult who had let his boundaries down.

It was normal to run into our students at the local deli. If they had permission to leave campus and were in good standing, they usually greeted me kindly. If they didn't, well, they were pretty easy to spot as they ducked into the chip aisle or hid behind a friend's backpack, making themselves far more obvious than if they had just said hello. On one occasion, I saw a girl climb into the trunk of a car and curl up while her friend slammed it shut—this was a new one for me. I stopped the car, which was full of five smiling teenagers, "Do you have permission to be down here?"

A choir of, "Yes, Mr. Bishop gave us permission."

"Did Mr. Bishop know you were going to put someone in your trunk?"

Another yes.

"Hmm . . . I'm going to guess no on that one. Can you please let her out? I will drive her back up, and I would like for all of us to meet with Mr. Bishop."

When we all gathered in the dining hall to sort through this situation, it became clear that there was nothing clear about the origins of this scenario.

Mr. Bishop said, "I told them yes for day students, no for boarding students."

The driver of the car insisted, "Wait . . . that's not true. You said if you're all day students (which we are, except Maddy), you can go, and then you said: 'I am supposed to say no to any boarders but then you raised your eyebrow and winked at us. So we just put Maddy in the trunk so no one would see. But then Mrs. Raney saw us."

Mr. Bishop was a top administrator at this school, and he had many years of experience in education. I was taken aback that he had found himself in this situation. Confused as to what I should do, and wanting to protect all feelings and allow the truth to come out, I let the girls leave and told them I would follow up later. Here is what Mr. Bishop had to say when we were one on one: "I'm sorry. I know. I have been saying no to students all weekend. I'm tired. I wanted a win. I just wanted to please someone. I wanted to say yes. Maddy has been having a tough week with grades and some disappointing college news. I felt bad for her. I know I should have said no. I just didn't. I had no idea they were going to put her in a trunk. But I do understand why they felt like I gave them permission to do that. I feel like an idiot."

Young people are looking for loopholes, and they are looking for what they want in the moment. I will repeat: *they want what they want in the moment.* They are not looking out for their future selves, they are looking to meet a need in the here and now. That is where we adults come in. And if we do not have solid, strong boundaries, when we are tired or find ourselves over-empathizing with a student, we may accidently let boundaries bend to the point of breaking. Tone and intention can change the delivery of these boundaries. Clear boundaries and clear communication of these boundaries are of equal importance in all relationships, but particularly in our work with youth.

Affection

"If you have a need for someone to unconditionally love you, get a puppy. That puppy will wag its tail and jump and even piss on the floor, it's so excited when you walk through the door. Students are not given to you to fill your void of unconditional love. I don't want to see anyone pissin' on the floor with excitement when you walk through the classroom door. They earn your respect by being prepared, attentive, and engaged, and you earn their trust by teaching, listening, and being reliable." This advice was delivered by a longtime principal to a group of new teachers. "Get a puppy." I love it.

I hear advice to new educators or coaches about being respected versus being liked. I have a problem with the dichotomy of that idea—that you have to be one or the other. I think it is a matter of what comes first. Work toward earning the respect of young people, not their admiration. It can be painful, as you will hear things like, "I love Mrs. Frias, she lets us out early from class all the time," or "Mr. Snyder is the best, if you go to him and cry, he will automatically bump up your grade," or "Ms. Mackey brings donuts to every class; she's so nice." This is buying children's affection. It's similar to the way some divorced parents unhealthily one-up the other by buying the newest video games to keep at their house. They figure that if they have a newer, cooler video game, their child will choose their house over the other parent's. Is that really how you want your child to grow up? Lured by the latest video game rather than a reliable, steady, and present parent? Gaining the admiration of young people is not a game, and it is not a competition.

I can see my own professional growth and my improvement in the area of establishing boundaries throughout my career as I look back at letters from students. And I can easily recall struggling to keep my desire for students' admiration in check.

Here is a letter from a student early in my career:

> *Yo Home-dawg Brooklyn,*
>
> *So I know you're not my real mom, but you've been referred to as my mother so many times I figured it would be completely inappropriate NOT to wish you a Happy Mother's Day. Plus, your birthday was on Wednesday, and I couldn't even celebrate with you, so this lame ass card is my way of making up for it* ☹
>
> *Anyway, I know in the past I have yelled at you, thrown objects at you, but that's really just my way of saying "I love you." Thank you so much for being here for me through all of my craziness, and I am seriously hoping to take you to college with me to hide under my bed and advise me for the next four years. And if that is not possible, then I hope you can visit me a sh*t ton! Sorry to end this heartfelt note with a swear word . . . .*
>
> *Love you,*
> *Lily*

Yikes. As someone studying and writing about boundaries, I am embarrassed to put this in print. But I reiterate: I have made mistakes in my career, and wish I had had the information and training then that I have now. I am in the trenches with you, and I recognize the intricacies of working with young people at this critical time in their lives, when so much feels like it is on the line. I know how much we care for our students, how badly we want to help them, and how easy it is for boundaries to get blurry if we don't mark them clearly and maintain them over time.

In the decade since I received this letter, my approach to education and to relating to young people has changed dramatically. Is it my age, my experiences, being burned, coming up short, succeeding, becoming educated on the topic, or becoming a mother myself that has changed my approach? Perhaps it's all of that? I recognize that everyone has to make their own path, but I hope in sharing these stories and tips I can help you avoid some of the potholes that tripped me up and wore me down.

Let's compare that first letter with another, which I received recently:

> *Dear Mrs. Raney,*
>
> *I will never be able to thank you enough for everything you did. I really couldn't have made it without you. I don't know how I'm going to make it through college without you as my advisor. I hope you know what an impact you have made on me, not just in my high school career, but in the person I am today. Thank you for always being there, and for being more like family than faculty. I will miss you so much!*
>
> *Love,*
>
> *Leah*
>
> *P.S. My mom wants to say something too:*
>
> *Brook,*
>
> *There are not enough words to say thank you, for all you did for Leah, and for all you did for me. Thank you for our partnership in raising this amazing girl. I am so thankful she had you to always be there for her. I will forever be grateful to you. Thank you again for watching out for my baby!*
>
> *Love,*
>
> *Karen*

As I sum up my thoughts on affection as it relates to boundaries, I am reminded of my time as a high school volunteer supervising recess at a local middle school. The principal said to me, "And if a kid tries to hug you, turn sideways so they end up bumping your hip and make it a side hug. We aren't allowed to front-to-front hug the students." As a student at an independent school, where hugging teachers was a part of daily life, this was hard for me to understand.

Different boundaries exist in different places with different people for different reasons. What is important is that you are aware of the rules and expectations for the specific organization you are working for, you respect them, and you fulfill them.

No matter what organization you work for, however, my strongest piece of advice is to let the letter you might get twenty years from now motivate you rather than the affection of the young person in front of you right now. By this, I mean that even educators need to refuel the tank, and need to be reminded that their work has impact. Let thoughts of your students' success, your athletes' progress, your campers' maturity, ten, fifteen, twenty years from now fill your tank. If you work toward admiration in the short term, you are doing it wrong. There is nothing better as an educator than hearing from a young person, when they are all grown up, letting you know that your work with them shaped the person they are today. Let this be what you work toward. That, and getting a puppy.

Telephone Game

Nothing has blurred the understanding of boundary lines more than technology. As youth interact more on their phones with their peers than they do in person, they begin expecting the same from the adults in their lives. This is a trend we must resist. At our school, my cell phone number was given to students to use in case of emergencies, which meant that students had my phone number to use at will.

I frequently received messages like this: "Mrs. Raney, I am having this issue with a friend, and it is not an emergency, but I still need to tell you about it and I need your help asap." The text would come in the evenings, on the weekends, and over breaks. I was always tempted to take the bait and begin counseling over the phone, but I knew this would do three things:

1. Soothe the student's anxiety through an artificial conversation in which neither of us had any ability to read tone or intention.
2. Reinforce the idea that I was the only adult who could help with this situation.
3. Break a boundary in my personal life; I needed and wanted to be attending to myself, my own child, and my family in my time off.

Over time and through experience (success and failure), I built the discipline to respond like this: "Not a good conversation for text. I try to keep my texting to emergencies or logistics. If you want to schedule a time to chat, send me some dates and times. Otherwise, if this isn't an emergency, and you feel comfortable, see if there is another adult on duty who you trust and can chat to about this."

This type of response protected my time, modeled boundary setting, and expressed trust in my colleagues. Fifty percent of the time I was met with, "I'll just wait and talk to you about it next week" and the other 50 percent of the time I got, "I'll go find Mr. X, I know he's on duty."

Needing students to need us, in order to validate our work and impact, is not healthy for anyone. Technology has upped the neediness factor by creating an expectation of instant reply and 24–7 accessibility. Texting is a casual form of communication, and it can imply a casual relationship. This can be detrimental to our role as a trusted adult.

With technology and social media, I would again urge you to understand your organization's stance and comply with it. Many schools have moved to specific online platforms through which teachers are instructed to communicate with students. School-sanctioned e-mail platforms as well as specialized notification and messaging apps provided by the school offer both surveillance and a record of all correspondence. This type of boundary setting can prevent blurriness and the sense of entitlement to 24–7 access, protecting students, educators, and organizations.

When social media was new, I did not see friending and following students as a problem. I believed it was our obligation to be part of their world, be role models, and have a clear understanding of what they were doing in this virtual space. As social media grew, I quickly learned the pitfalls of following and friending students and of them following and friending me and other adults in supervisory roles:

1. Like texting, social media following suggests a more casual relationship.
2. Material you post for your adult friends may not be in precise alignment with the values of the organization or institution you work for, and may set a bad example for young people in your care or contradict your role.
3. Social media relationships can create an impression of favoritism—who gets to follow, who doesn't, what they see, and so on. I actually had a student say to me, "Mrs. Jacobson always snaps Zach back immediately but then leaves me unread. And Zach gets A's in her class and I get C's. Clearly, it's favoritism."
4. What you see online is as reportable as what you see or hear in person. When you follow students or allow them to follow you, you are extending your job to 24–7 responsibility.
5. You are connecting your professional world very closely to your personal world, and students may find out more than you want them to through the information you post or what your followers post and share.

It's important that we adults know how social media works and are aware of the ways teens are using it. I believe that adult family members and guardians should be connected to their kids' social media profiles and supervising their children's activity online. But this is not the role of the trusted adult outside the family who is working with the child in a formal capacity.

The Shoulder Test

When you are the trusted adult in a relationship with a young person, it's critical to remember that *you are always the adult*. The roles don't reverse, and you can't suspend your position as the mature, experienced person. This does not mean you have to have all the answers; as we discussed earlier, vulnerability and the phrase "I don't know" are powerful tools for building trust. However, being the adult does mean that you are the one responsible. Your priority must always be the health and safety of the young people in your care.

With this responsibility comes power; in many relationships with adults, there is something a child can gain or earn—a grade, playing time, a badge, or your approval. You must take this power seriously and check yourself frequently. As much as young people challenge us, they have an underlying need to please. As we get to know students, especially on a boarding school campus, we interact and transact outside our classrooms or the particular setting of the formal relationship. For example—and this example is specific to boarding schools—you might make requests of students you know for babysitting, dog walking, plant watering, or other general chores. Young people might ask you (or other adults) for food, rides to the bus station, to watch a game at your house, and so on. It is important that you offer opportunities to multiple young people in your care, and that you do not rely on the same young people over and over. You should also make sure to pay students for their time and their work. These practices ensure that motives are not questioned, and that interactions are not seen as favors with a payback somewhere down the line. Instead, these are straightforward transactions for services.

Inevitably, in our work with young people, conflict will arise. A young person will lie to you. A young person will do the opposite of what you asked them to do. A young person will harm the experience of another young person in your care. These slipups are not a direct reflection of you and your effectiveness in your role. When conflict occurs and trust is broken, maintain appropriate boundaries, and pause to reflect.

Check Yourself

Conflicts with young people are inevitable. Usually, clashes occur when an adult is asking the young person to do something they don't want to do or are having a hard time doing (picking up after themselves, keeping their hands to themselves, treating others with dignity, etc.). When moments like this occur and young people push back, it is difficult not to take their behavior personally—and therefore it is difficult not to react from a personal place. Instead, take a mindful moment, check in with yourself, and reflect on the following questions:

1. Is the action I am witnessing the teenage brain at work? *This question will help you put into perspective what is in the young person's control and what isn't. Either way, they should be held accountable, but reminding yourself of the growing adolescent brain, and the attendant growing pains, can help you understand the behavior at play.*

2. Is my reaction for me or for the young person? *Am I trying to meet any of my needs through this child right now? Pause to check in and reflect on what else is going on in your life,*

and how your feelings and emotions are playing out in this moment. Maybe you just received a negative performance review, maybe you had a fight with your spouse, maybe you found out a good friend is ill. Real-life triggering factors can change the way we might normally react.

3. What is motivating the student right now? *Understanding the need the student is meeting by acting this way can help you form your response and address the problem rather than the symptom.*

4. What is motivating me right now? *Does the action of the student strike a particular nerve with you for personal reasons? In other words, might another adult in this young person's life respond differently? What is it that I really want?*

In any conflict, we have the opportunity to pour gasoline on the spark and really light it up! We also have the opportunity to grab the fire extinguisher and work to put that flame out. We know that greater growth and development can occur when we take the latter approach. By hitting the pause button to check in on our thoughts and reflect on our feelings, we can better recognize our own personal head space and control the way our own high school experiences, our own egos, and our own current life events influence our actions. This gained perspective on our emotions helps us to plan an effective response to young people's behavior.

The first step to checking, reflecting, and responding effectively to conflict is the sometimes difficult task of admitting your true feelings. I was taught this lesson, and reassured that vulnerability and asking for help is the answer, when a new teacher came to unload in my office. I was serving in a mentor role for her, and on one particular afternoon she unexpectedly arrived in my office to share that a girl in her class had been bullying the others. I asked what she had done to address the situation so far. Here is what she said: "I'm ashamed to admit I haven't done anything. And honestly, it's because I'm scared. She looks just like a girl in my high school who tortured me for four years. I'm scared if I meet with her one on one I'll either break down crying or I'll slap her. I need your help."

Clearly, this educator had some unpacking of her own high school experience to do, but I was glad that she brought the issue forward and asked for help. Again, you will not always be the right adult to deal with every situation, and seeking the help of trusted colleagues is key.

Recognizing your power, checking and reflecting, and grabbing the fire extinguisher in moments of conflict can assist in setting boundaries—and so can the shoulder test. If there is one thing you remember from this book, let it be this: In every interaction you have with a young person, imagine your supervisor sitting and observing from your right shoulder and the parents of the child doing the same on your left shoulder. If these figures would approve of your actions, your words, and your tone and intention, you are most likely acting within the healthy and clear boundaries of your role. If they would pause or question, so should you.

To enhance the image further, when practicing your shoulder test, add a GoPro on the forehead of the young person you are interacting with, a bystander filming on a smartphone, and four surveillance cameras pointed in your direction from every angle. Would you want footage of this interaction to go viral? I do not say this to simply intensify the metaphor but to inspire you to consistently and reliably act with recognition of your power, with the child's best interest in mind, and within a healthy, clear, established set of boundaries.

CHAPTER 9

Upholding Boundaries at the Organizational Level

Setting healthy and clear boundaries with young people is the responsibility of individual professionals, yet it can be difficult to do this effectively without the support and full attention of the organization. The *Journal of Child Sexual Abuse, 2018,* reported that, "A nationwide study of school superintendents, principals, child sex abuse experts, and attorneys who prosecute or defend school sex abusers identified 100 actions in five categories that they believe, with 80 percent or more agreement, would lead to prevention and/or reduction of child sexual abuse by employees in schools. The categories are policies, hiring, training, supervision, and reporting. Most of these actions that were identified are already part of expected practice in schools but may not be carried out."

Leaders, including board members, of all organizations that serve young people must screen rigorously when hiring employees and enlisting volunteers. It is imperative that all leaders be held to the highest standards for knowing and following the law; and when responding to reports of abuse, they must act promptly and with compassion, and utilize trauma-informed practices. The leaders set the tone for employees and volunteers, and they are squarely responsible for the importance and priority placed on child safety at their organization. This is a weighty responsibility, but with continual conversations and training it need not be a burden.

Clarity and regularity should be a team's motto when it comes to organizational standards for setting boundaries. There should be a clear understanding of, and written documents backing, the organization's job descriptions and policies. There should also be clarity surrounding the practice of one-on-one time with young people and reporting responsibilities. These policies and practices make up the cultural cornerstones of the organization and should be reviewed and revised with regularity. Throughout this chapter, we'll look at things to consider when setting up spaces for your teams to work safely and effectively with young people. Whether you are in a role that can effect large organizational change or you are in the trenches doing the daily work with youth, it is important for your safety and protection, as well as the youth in your care, to take a special interest in the general policies and practices of the organization.

Job Descriptions Are Not Suggestions

In the educational world, job descriptions can become something of a joke among colleagues, because they know that there is always far more to do than a list of responsibilities could ever encapsulate. What is worrisome for an educator is the "duties as assigned" clause often found at the end of the job description, which leaves us open to be asked to do anything! But this lack of clarity in job descriptions is also dangerous for organizations and for youth—the absence of limits can create a gray area where adults can operate outside of their domains in which they are trained. When job descriptions are not specifically outlined, or are so out of date or irrelevant that they are not taken seriously, employees may begin working beyond their zone of expertise.

Let's imagine the school secretary and the history teacher swapped roles. Or the camp counselor and head cook exchanged jobs for a day. Or the librarian and grounds crew traded responsibilities. Maybe the lawn would get cut but wouldn't look as good as it normally does. And the camp meals might not get out on time or taste as good. And the library books may not get returned and recorded according to protocol. Although we could survive for a while, things would eventually start to fall apart and services would not be delivered to the desired standard.

These are all low-stakes examples. But what if a teacher played mental health professional for the day? What might happen then? As savvy and experienced as I think I am in my work with youth, I have not had one conversation with a school counselor where I did not learn something. Social workers, counselors, therapists, psychologists, health professionals, and others have skills and expertise that I don't have. I must stay within my realm and support them in theirs, and they will do the same for me. Some youth-serving organizations have figured out the importance of clearly articulated and specific job descriptions the hard way, and, unfortunately, to the detriment of the youth in their care.

A director of a coed middle and high school summer camp shared with me a difficult situation he encountered a few years ago. He had just taken the job as director after many years at a similar camp nearby. He had plenty of experience, and was eager to take on this leadership role. The director he was replacing was a woman who had been at the camp since its founding. The board thought it would be helpful to keep her around as an assistant to the director, with minimal formal responsibilities, to serve in an advisory role.

The truth was, she had not been performing up to standards in her last couple of years as director, but the board was hesitant to terminate her, as she had such a legacy in the organization. Without meaningful consultation with the new director, and given her years of experience, the board allowed the previous director to begin her new role without a clear job description—she just floated through camp doing whatever she wanted to do. The new director, who was sharing this story with me, said he figured, what real harm could she do? She checked in with the waterfront people in the morning, did some archery in the afternoon, and attended all the meals. He reported that her presence didn't seem to be helping or hurting, she was just there.

This all seemed to hold true until about halfway through the six-week camp, when the director received an e-mail from a parent that they were on their way to pick up their child. In the e-mail the parent shared that the former director had recommended to the family that they come pick up their child. Confused, the new director went to get some answers.

"Riley's parents said they are on their way to pick her up, and mentioned your name. Any idea why?" She responded with pride, "Yes, I've been taking care of this one. Riley came to me a couple weeks ago and said she felt like she wasn't fitting in. She hadn't made any friends. I let her move out of the cabin and in with me for the time being, and I have been counseling her in the evenings."

"Are you a counselor?"

"No, but I have plenty of experience. I don't need a fancy piece of paper to tell me how to work with kids. I've been doing it my whole life. I let Riley's parents know that she is suffering from OCD and anxiety. There are other camps that specialize in that sort of thing, so I gave them some recommendations. They are on their way to get her."

The new director was at a loss for words. He now had a former director—who had been underperforming—allowing a camper to stay in her cabin, counseling the girl in the evenings, and recommending that she leave camp, all without consulting any health professional or other camp leaders.

Unfortunately, stories like this are common. The well-meaning employee may be young, old, have little experience, have plenty of experience—it doesn't matter; employees in youth-serving organizations take pride in the way they serve young people, even if their actions are sometimes outside their job description, or even the law. Often, they believe so wholeheartedly in their own good intentions and the rightness of their actions that they cannot see the unintended consequences. They believe they are going "above and beyond" in the best interest of the child, but too often their underlying objective is to fill their own need to feel needed, and their actions are misguided.

We each have a responsibility to work positively with young people, but each of us brings a certain set of qualifications, credentials, and expertise to the team. When people work beyond their scope, they may accidently do harm while attempting to do good. Organizations must set up proper reporting chains so that employees know when, where, and to whom they should take important information, so that people with the right qualifications can handle sensitive situations. Then, organizations need to repeatedly train on this protocol, and individuals need to listen up.

Not Your Rules to Make or Break

The phrase, "I know that the rule says this . . . but I expect this . . ." is one of the most detrimental phrases to the boundaries you have established with young people. I believe in meeting individual needs whenever possible, while staying fair and true to the mission and values of an organization. When individuals stray from the policies of an organization, they create a terrifying boundaryless world for the young people we serve. Even if youth resist the rules, they crave consistency, predictability, and clarity. When teachers take "matters into their own hands," they promote a lack of trust in the organization, and, often, unforeseen consequences result, as exemplified in the next story.

A family told me about a school experience that was particularly detrimental to their son's self-esteem. On the first day of class, his history teacher said, "I know the school says that if you are absent from class I will provide you with the materials you missed—that is not the case in this classroom. I won't. My job is to prepare you for college, and you aren't going to get any handouts in college. I also know that if you are tardy, I am supposed to mark it so, and so many tardies will add up to an absence, and those absences will add up to detentions. I can't stand complicated and delayed systems like this, so I do it my own way. If you are absent, I don't mark you that way, you just get an F for the day and your grade will suffer. If you are tardy, you need to do five push-ups for every minute you are late. I have found my method works much better for attendance than the ridiculous school policy. My way of operating is not for you to share with any other teachers, this is a deal between you and me." The parents and the administration were unaware of this policy until the following situation occurred.

After the first quarter this young man, who had straight A's in all his other classes, came home with his first F in a class. His parents sat him down to ask if he needed a tutor or if there was anything else they could do to support him. They went through his student portal and found A's on all his tests in the class, so the issue was not one of understanding content. As the parents dug further, here is what the boy hesitantly revealed:

"I missed a few classes, and that's why I got an F."

"But your attendance record reports that you have perfect attendance," his parents replied.

"He doesn't work like that."

"What do you mean he doesn't work like that?"

"Well, on Mondays, Wednesdays, and Fridays I have wood shop at the other end of the school. We always get let out late, and we have to change. I was late on the first Monday for this class, and had to do fifteen push-ups."

"Push-ups?"

"His policy is that you have to do five push-ups for every minute you are late. I was three minutes late. He does this so he doesn't have to report us as tardy or absent. It's embarrassing, because I couldn't even do fifteen push-ups, and the class watches while you do it, and he made fun of me. So, on Mondays, Wednesdays, and Fridays, if I am going to be late, I just go to the cafeteria instead and I study the chapter we are working on in class. He doesn't mark me absent, he just gives me an F for the day. I know the material, but the F's for a day add up. And now I'm failing."

You can see where this situation is going. When we operate outside our scope and make our own rules, we end up undermining the overarching vision and mission rather than supporting it. The result is complete chaos and confusion rather than the needed safety of consistency and clarity.

"Do what you say, and say what you do" is a phrase lawyers have repeated at educational and camp leadership conferences I have attended. Your policies must match your practice and your practice must match your policies. You have been hired to uphold the standards of the organization you work for. It is only fair that the organization keep their job descriptions, policies, and procedures up to date and they train and inform you on their expectations for you in your specific role. Then, you must work within those guardrails. If you question a decision or a standing policy, you should raise it in the appropriate forum—and every organization should have a process through which your concerns can be discussed and addressed. Your questioning or disapproval of a policy should never be raised in the midst of an issue, or within eyesight or earshot of a young person you are working with. A united front, supportive colleagues, and an organizational leadership team open to feedback are crucial to creating a safe and secure environment for young people.

Handling One-on-One Time

One-on-one time with young people is a difficult and important dilemma to tackle: while our most impactful and important trust-building work with young people happens in one-on-one settings, so does the majority of abuse. An organization called Darkness to Light, which focuses on ending child abuse, reports that "More than 80% of sexual abuse cases occur in isolated, one-on-one situations." If the danger of potential criminal violations causes us to lose the ability to work one on one with young people, I worry about our ability to build trusted relationships with young people, and about both the feasibility and economics of important programs. If we had to double the number of people who run programs, the cost might be too great to sustain and kids will lose opportunities.

During my son's regular school day, he is alone with an adult who is not a parent at least three to four times a day: drum lessons, theater tech, math tutoring, and the school bus. That's just a regular day. It is imperative, in our current setup, that we trust adults to be alone with him if he is to get the most out of his educational and extracurricular experiences. I would also argue that, being one on one in drum lessons is a crucial factor in the trust he has built with Jared, his instructor, and the important discussions they have had that reach well beyond beats and tempo.

The National Association of Independent Schools comments on the issue of one-on-one time in a document titled *Prevention and*

Response: Recommendations for Independent School Leaders from the Independent School Task Force on Educator Sexual Misconduct. This document, provided to the association's member schools, advises that "In general, schools should strive to keep student interactions with adults readily interruptible and observable. This means that students interacting with an adult are, or could be, within hearing or visual range of another adult and/or other students generally."

The recommendations acknowledge that this is not always possible. If a boarding school student needs to go to an appointment, for instance, should two adults go? The paper states that risk needs to be managed, and when it's not possible for the situation to be observable and interruptible, other measures—such as a detailed schedule of the trip and check-ins of adult and student upon return—can be put in place to reduce risk and ensure safety.

Guidelines for One-on-One Time

Darkness to Light published the following guidance regarding the one-on-one time young people are experiencing with adults. The piece is directed to parents, but it is important for trusted adults to practice as well.

ONE-ON-ONE TIME with trusted adults is healthy and valuable for a child. It builds self-esteem and deepens relationships. To protect children while nurturing these relationships:
- Drop in unexpectedly when the child is alone with an adult or another youth, even if it is a trusted family member.
- Make sure outings are observable—if not by you, then by others.
- Ask adults about the specifics of planned activities before the child leaves your care. Notice their ability to be specific.

- Talk with the child following the activity. Notice the child's mood and whether he or she can tell you with confidence how the time was spent.
- Find a way to tell adults who care for children that you and the child are educated about child sexual abuse. Be that direct.

In my position as a parent and educator, I am seeing a wider gap between trusted adults and parents, which is arising because of our greater reliance on technology. As an educator, even just ten years ago, when my students and players were being picked up from the dorm or from the rink after hockey practice, I used to interact with parents far more frequently because they would get out of their car and come into the building to let their child know they were there. Today, parents sit in their car and text the child that they are waiting outside. The child jumps up to end their activity, exclaims "my mom's here," exits the building, gets in the car, and no interaction between parent and the supervising adult takes place.

Because of the research I have done and the horror stories I have read of abuse, which has only increased my desire to know the other adults in my son's life, I behave quite differently as a parent. I always get out of the car, enter the building, and greet the adult. This builds a bridge between me and my child, as I show an interest in how he is spending his time, and between me and his teacher or instructor, as I let them know I am an attentive parent.

There is a line to walk here, of course, in allowing your child to express independence and at the same time keep your child safe. I am in no way encouraging parents to be helicopter parents who fly in at a moment's notice to "save" their child, and inevitably interfere with learning. I am simply advocating that parents take the available opportunities to connect with the trusted adults in their child's life, so they can look each other in the eyes and commit to the well-being of the child in their common care. I highly encourage trusted adults and youth-serving organizations to find ways to make their spaces interruptible and observable—invite people in—for the protection of both the adults and the kids. I also encourage organizations to generate a conversation with their teams about one-on-one work with youth. It is imperative that organizations set and communicate clear standards. The expectations must be named, the exceptions should be identified, and scenarios should be rehearsed that plainly demonstrate best practices as determined by the organization.

Reporting Responsibilities

There are boundary violations, and then there is abuse. A participant in one of my trainings commented, "I just think that having to train adults on boundaries is ridiculous. You're the adult. They are the child. What is to teach?" I understand her frustration. If proper boundary setting is so clear for her, why isn't it clear for others? I recognize that this book will likely not change the mind of a criminal intent on abusing a child, but I do hope that it helps well-intentioned adults set appropriate boundaries with young people, so that young people know and feel what proper boundaries look like. When they experience the firm and healthy boundaries established by the trustworthy adults in their lives, they can better gauge if they are in a dangerous situation with a dangerous adult. I also hope that this book informs trusted adults on the signs of abuse and what to do if they suspect a child is being abused.

Darkness to Light: Recognize the Signs

Don't expect obvious signs when a child is being sexually abused. Signs are often present, but you have to know what to look for. Emotional and behavioral signs or changes are common and can include:
• Anxiety and depression
• Sleep disturbances, including nightmares or night terrors
• Change in eating habits
• Unusual fear of certain people or places; reluctance to be alone with a certain person
• Changes in mood that could including anger, aggressiveness toward parents, siblings, friends, pets
• Rebellion or withdrawal; runaway behavior
• Change in attitude toward school or academic performance; lack of interest in friends, sports, or other activities
• Unexplained or frequent health problems like headaches or stomachaches
• Poor self-esteem; avoidance of relationships
• Self-mutilation or change in body perception, like thinking of self or body as dirty or bad; suicidal thoughts
• Regression to previously outgrown behaviors, for example bedwetting or thumb-sucking
• Abnormal sexual behaviors or knowledge of advanced sexual language and behaviors
• Too "perfect" behavior or overly compliant behavior

In our trainings as educational leaders, we are taught that the first place a victim looks for support is in the handbook of the school or organization. If you are like me, you inherited a handbook, manual, policies and/or procedures, and, as someone who is eager to get to work with the young people in your care, the last thing you wanted to work on was a handbook revision. I pursued a career in education because I loved working with young people, not because I loved reviewing and editing policies. Just months into the dean of students job, I'd already had two or three parents and students come to me saying, "But in your handbook it says you..." I began to understand how important it is to do what we say and say what we do. People rely on printed text for direction, security, and predictability, and it is the responsibility of the organization to provide it.

One of the most important items to have in print, and to train your staff on regularly, is your state's mandated reporting responsibility. Some states require those in certain professions to report suspicion of abuse, while other states require this of all citizens. The government-run information service Child Welfare Information Gateway has an accessible database in which you can search every state's mandated reporting responsibility law.

Mandatory Reporting Law

Each state has its own statutes regarding mandatory reporting of suspicions of child abuse or neglect, and it is critical that you be familiar with the reporting requirements of the state in which you live or work. As an example, here is the relevant law in New Hampshire:

Citation: Rev. Stat. § 169-C:29
The following professionals are required to report:
- Physicians, surgeons, county medical examiners, psychiatrists, residents, interns, dentists, osteopaths, optometrists, chiropractors, nurses, hospital personnel, or Christian Science practitioners
- Teachers, school officials, nurses, or counselors

- Day care workers or any other child or foster care workers
- Social workers
- Psychologists or therapists
- Priests, ministers, or rabbis
- Law enforcement officials

Citation: Rev. Stat. § 169-C:29
All other persons who have reason to suspect that a child has been abused or neglected must report.
Citation: Rev. Stat. § 169-C:29
A report is required when a person has reason to suspect that a child has been abused or neglected.

As you can see, the statute calls out specific professions as mandated reporters but then makes an inclusive statement for all other persons who suspect neglect or abuse.

When I began facilitating trainings at different schools on trusted adults and boundaries, I would plan for a reminder of mandated reporting as one of my many topics, but the training was never meant to be chiefly about reporting responsibilities. Inevitably, at each training, a teacher would raise their hand and say, "What is a mandated reporting responsibility?" This would derail the conversation for a solid half hour while the administrators made defensive statements like, "Don't you remember when we did that training last year? And also, it's in your faculty handbook." I would defuse the situation by looking up the law in that state and, in front of the large group, informing the team of the legal requirement and giving the leaders the task of training the entire team twice a year and all new employees/volunteers upon hiring. I have learned my lesson, and in my current capacity in partnership with schools, I require that the faculty and staff be reminded of their mandated reporting responsibilities before I conduct my training.

There are many obstacles that get in the way of mandated reporter training: employee turnover, absent board leadership, crisis management, time. Many organizations have failed to train their staff regularly for understandable reasons, but there is no excuse.

I strongly recommend that your organization designate key people who are specifically trained and identified by the team to serve as specialists of mandated reporting responsibilities and trauma-informed practices. The best people for this role are often nurses, counselors, HR officers, and Student or Residential Life staff. I also recommend that you never expect a trusted adult on your team to make a report alone. As organizational leaders, you want to be aware if a report is being made from your organization, and you also want your team to feel supported, especially during the toughest of scenarios. By creating a reporting chain and training your team, you can ensure that a report never happens without the knowledge of the organizational leaders, and that your team always feels they have the support they need.

The employee in your organization who is aware of, or suspects, the neglect or abuse of a young person should be expected to report to their supervisors. From there, the reporting chain should be utilized, and a specialized team should gather to agree on a plan. In most states, when the information is deemed reportable, the employee who had firsthand awareness and knowledge of abuse is responsible for making the report. Again, I recommend that this is done together as a team, while meeting all state laws and mandates.

In cases where an organizational leader is one of the named abusers, the employee should always make a direct report to the children's welfare organization in their state. The bottom line is that, in order to keep young people safe, and to protect yourself as an adult from civil and criminal liability, it is crucial that you are aware of the standards of reporting in your state, and that you report within the timeframe your state requires. Organizations must make training on mandated reporting a top priority.

The same policy that applies at airports should apply to youth-serving organizations: If you see something, say something. Here is another way to think through individual responsibilities and to train your teams how to use gut, guts, and gusto to do the right thing.

> **Gut**: If you witness or hear of something that does not feel right in your gut, it probably isn't. Using your intuition, asking questions, and carefully observing the behavior of other adults is an important part of preventing or stopping neglect and abuse. If you witness adults giving extra gifts or flattering a young person, actively seeking time alone, using secrets as a way to build a relationship, or using manipulative behavior with the young person or their family, the alarm in your gut should go off.
>
> **Guts**: It takes guts to speak up when your intuition tells you something isn't right. In a later chapter, we will discuss building a colleague-to-colleague feedback culture that reinforces the courage to speak up and assists in keeping appropriate boundaries in place. In the moment of witnessing what is potentially abuse, neglect, or grooming, however, you do not have to be concerned about having all of the facts, or 100 percent conviction; you should simply share with a supervisor or your designated report when something doesn't feel right. Then, you should follow up to inquire what they have done with that information.
>
> **Gusto**: Living your life with gusto is key to developing strong intuition and the courage to speak up when something isn't right. Going for the gusto means living loud and proud, and speaking up about right and wrong. Hypocrites are a danger

to any culture, but in order to call out hypocrisy you must be professional in establishing your boundaries with young people as well as serving as a role model and leader in the work beyond your paid profession. When you punch out and your official work ends for the day, young people are still watching, looking for a role model like you. Living with gusto means being an active part of the greater culture—in the case of a trusted adult, defending against abuse and neglect, keeping young people safe, and supporting and encouraging them in all areas of your life.

Tragedy

If there is one thing I know for sure about boundaries, it is the necessity of individuals and organizations setting them when times are easy and when relationships are new. I learned this through experience. In 2016, I was a dorm parent for a dorm of five sophomore and junior girls. Our dorm was at the bottom of the hill on which the school sat and farthest from the dining hall and academic buildings; it was also the smallest dorm on campus. Girls chose to be in this dorm for a reason, and it wasn't the long climb up a steep incline every morning. Their desire to be in this dorm typically came from a connection to me, a preventative move on their part to live close to the dean, and because they enjoyed the small family-like environment that a dorm of five could provide.

In my administrative role, I found myself working more often with adults and felt pulled away from the daily work I loved to do with students. The dorm was where I felt most connected and happiest in my work. Because of this, and the small size of the dorm, boundaries were light. The girls would flow freely from my kitchen to the dorm, making themselves mac and cheese and snuggling our family's dogs. I was on duty four nights a week, which was an organizational mistake. Most faculty members did one to two nights of duty a week. We had under-hired that year and, letting down my boundaries and working beyond the scope of my job description (I thought for the betterment of the team and the kids), I agreed I should take on more.

Because I was on duty so often, the girls came to feel I was on duty all the time. We spent so much time together that I came to trust them quickly. They trusted me back. They called me "mom," and I took too much pride in our close relationships. Our way of operating worked, but it was not organizationally or personally sustainable. My lack of self-care and the organization's encouragement to always do more led to boundary-bend, and when tragedy struck, the boundaries broke.

In October 2016, one of the girls in my dorm left for the weekend and never returned. She went home to Vermont and attended a concert with four friends. On their drive home, a man driving the wrong way on I-89 struck them head on. All five teenagers, from the same Vermont town, died in the crash. Our dorm of five became a dorm of four, and the world and our school lost an incredibly vibrant, driven, and kind young woman.

This was the most difficult time I have ever faced as an educator. Too many of you, unfortunately, know how it feels to lose a student. The greatest struggle becomes the need to grieve yourself while supporting and guiding your students through their grief. I got lost in this push-pull. My dorm "mom" role as well as my dean role—in which I felt ultimate responsibility for making sure the rest of the children were okay—mixed with my own sense of terrible loss for a girl I so admired, left me swirling.

The second greatest difficulty was navigating the "grief competition" that comes with the loss of a student. This was something a colleague at another school had warned me about, but I had no idea how powerful the phenomenon could be. When a student dies, there is silent battle within the school over who was closest or bestest of friends, and this creates a hierarchy of who is allowed to mourn the hardest and the loudest. It may sound silly, but the experience is real and it is important to address.

In the dorm, I let up on the rules and the boundaries even further. I felt so terribly for these four girls, for their loss, for my inability to find the right things to say, and for my failure to save them from having to face a tragedy like this one. But looser boundaries are not what these girls needed. Looking back, I see that these adolescents who were suffering craved normalcy and boundaries. They were seeking support, but needed to be held accountable. Hearing, "Do whatever you need" and being given free passes for behavior that had previously been unacceptable was confusing, and impossible for them to navigate. One girl ended up leaving the dorm, and the dynamics among the three remaining were unsettled and uncomfortable. We limped through to the end of the year. Given the benefit of hindsight, greater experience, and more training, I would have done so much differently and I would have asked more of my organization—a more appropriate work setup, tasks, and commitment within my job description, more training on boundaries and what to do during potential tragedy on the front end, and much more support in upholding boundaries on the back end.

Boundaries are not punishments, they are safety. Knowing where the line is provides security. Organizations need to create a team understanding of what boundaries are and why they are important. It is also key to help adults recognize that boundaries will be tested, and sometimes these tests come through tragedy. In New England, we put up a snow fence before the snow arrives. Coastal states prone to hurricanes don't wait to build sandbag barricades until the tide begins to rise. It is impossible to construct the fence or barricade *after* the onslaught of snow or water starts. We know it is coming, and we must prepare for it. The old adage "Plan for the worst and hope for the best" holds true in organizational boundary-setting work with youth. We work with hundreds or thousands of young people, who have families all over the country or even scattered across the world; being connected to this many people means there will be tragedy. Unforeseen circumstances will bend the boundaries, and organizations need to be prepared if they are to prevent the boundary from breaking.

Providing clear and up-to-date job descriptions, editing policy and keeping the team informed of changes, and training on mandated reporting responsibilities, all before the test of tragedy, will set your organization up for success. An equal amount of responsibility relies on the organization and the individuals to keep young people safe. Now we can shift focus to proactively building a culture within your organization that supports the work of trust and boundary building.

Part III
Creating Culture

CHAPTER 10

Partnering with Purpose

Building a culture is a sacred endeavor, whether that culture exists one hour a week, as in a weekly after-school enrichment program, or 24–7, as in a boarding school. When entering into an established culture, you don't necessarily consider how it came to be. Who were the influencers and how did they decide what would be right and wrong, good or bad in this particular environment? But when we become part of an organization, we certainly sense a culture unique to the space, time, and people. As you visit schools, camps, churches, homes, teams, anywhere a culture is being built, you can feel the differences among them. You begin to absorb the norms of each, and you quickly learn what is okay to say, wear, or do. Daniel Coyle, author of *The Culture Code*, says exactly that: "Culture is a set of living relationships working toward a shared goal. It's not something you are. It's something you do."

Though I've been part of many educational institutions, I was never hyperaware of visible culture, hidden culture, or the impact of traditions on culture until I founded a summer camp. When you join an organization, you typically learn the culture and live in it without thinking too much about it. You follow the rest of the flock. That all changes when you are the leader, making decisions in the moment that will influence the future of the culture. Until you are in that spot, it is difficult to fathom the responsibility that comes with big decisions, as well as some seemingly small ones. I remember a camper saying to me, "It's Tuesday, we always have pizza on Tuesday. Why isn't there pizza?" When I responded that I was unaware of that tradition, and that this was only the second year of camp, she shared that this was actually her first year, but she had heard from other girls that we always had pizza on Tuesdays and that this was a tradition that should be taken seriously. Of course, the weight of decisions that build culture are far greater than pizza. I have had to put stakes in the ground for our position on technology, use of time, diversity, sustainability, roommates, relationships, rules, budget, and who and what we celebrate, to name a few. Many of the decisions, large and small, that we make daily as leaders cause actions and reactions in our people, and these in time shape the culture of the community.

Typically, the young people in our care are only with us for a short period in comparison to the history of the organization. But the adolescents begin to create and craft traditions of their own and draw conclusions about events that occur. A colleague of mine used to say, "It happened once so it's a school tradition." Once you become aware of this tendency and are actively observing the growth and change of a culture, it is fascinating to note what norms live on, and what ends when people move on.

Hardy Girls, Healthy Women, an impactful organization based in Maine, writes about young people as plants. When a plant does not thrive, we do not blame the seed—we look to the environment and surroundings to understand what went wrong. Trusted adults such as teachers and coaches typically enter into a young person's journey when they are already half grown. So, without any control over where the seed was planted, what kind of soil it lived in, and how much sunlight and water the seedling was given in its early stages, the trusted adult is expected to help the growing plant thrive. This is a tall order, particularly given the number of risks young people face today.

Transplanting the roots from the original soil into the soil and culture of your organization is a delicate process. Equally important is the curating and attention given to the growing of a team of trusted adults. The *Role of the Trusted Adult*, a study out of Australia, found that, while relationships between adults and young people cannot be manufactured, "from a policy perspective conditions could be enabled or created to help facilitate trusting relationships between young people and adults." It reports further that "while this may sometimes occur via formal mentoring, trusted adult relationships could also be supported through fostering community structures where young people can meet and get to know adults from different parts of the community or by supporting the adults who surround young people to implement the low-key, direct, and equitable communication that young people value." Teams of trusted adults can be coached and built, and so, too, can partnerships with graduates of our programs, leaders of local organizations, and parents. We can also encourage student-to-student partnerships, all with the purpose of developing and maintaining a healthy culture that supports growth.

Say It, Do It, and Become It

Growing up in a small town, my brother, sister, and I said hello to everyone we passed, and our parents trained us to make eye contact. The banker, the baker, the postmaster, the stranger on the street, it didn't matter, you said hello with eye contact and a little nod. You can imagine me living in New York City for a year while in graduate school, saying hello to everyone I encountered on the train, on the street, at the coffee shop. People thought I was nuts!

But it was a habit I'd developed in the culture I grew up in. It was just what we did.

In high school, I remember visiting a friend in Michigan for a weekend. We went to the grocery store and I saw tipped-over shopping carts all over the parking lot. I quickly started turning them upright and rolling them to their return spot. My friend yelled, "What are you doing?" I said, "There must have been a storm or something, I'm just going to help pick up a few of these carts." She looked at me, puzzled, and when she and her mom finished loading their groceries into the car, they tipped their cart over onto the grass near their parking spot. Now I looked puzzled. In this particular town, when you are done with your cart you just tip it over on the lawn so it doesn't blow away, and someone who works there will pick it up. My parents would have been mortified if I had done that. We always return our carts. That was an expectation in our community. In this community, it wasn't. How did that come to be? And how hard would it be to change?

I worked with a group of students who were frustrated with their school's lack of school spirit. Really, they were frustrated with an all-around lack of desire to be at that school on the part of both the adults and the students. The culture lacked commitment, enthusiasm, drive, and connectedness, as identified by the students. I ran them through an exercise where we named the things that were within the control of this small group of students and things that were not within their control. They also identified the way their culture was described in writing, such as on their website and social media feeds, in their school handbook, on signs around the hallways, and so on. By their account, the stated values of the school did not match the day-to-day practices at the school. They chose to make a list of actions that did align with the words and themes the school supposedly embraced, and each student committed to performing these actions for one week. They listed such things as expressing gratitude to a teacher, celebrating another student, wearing clothing in the school colors, and creating a super-fan award of candy for the loudest and most enthusiastic student at the upcoming basketball game.

A week later I checked in with them, and they arrived at our meeting with five more students—and many more ideas. Each week, the group listed their weekly intentions, went out and completed them, and came back for a check-in, energy boost, and new set of intentions. The small group of change makers slowly grew to a big group of change makers, and after a year, with no quantitative data to prove it, I can qualitatively say that the group shifted and reshaped the school's culture from within. The partnership of these students and the impact of their positive actions were immediately visible through a rise in attendance at school events and a decrease in class absences. Proven through surveys over time, students reported feeling happier, more engaged, and safer at school. Teachers and administrators credited this positive swing to the hard work and commitment of these student leaders.

Since that big moment, I have witnessed or heard about many other student-driven initiatives that positively changed cultures that did not fully support their needs. I have heard of students partnering to propose and push for the hiring of a school counselor; a redesign of their all-community meetings to give students more leadership opportunities; clubs and activities that planned events during times of high risk for youth substance use and abuse, mainly after school and in the evenings; development and delivery of consent education and sexual assault prevention; and a student survey to check in on the happiness and engagement of their peers. All of these initiatives were led by students and aimed at improving culture.

The greatest lesson learned by watching these incredible students work, was that if they make a pledge and start acting on it, the cultural change will follow. If student leaders say, "We are respectful, spirited, and kind," hang signs all over school that repeat this idea, and then outwardly act in this way with full confidence and conviction, they can slowly align their school culture with their vision. As trusted adults in such situations, our role is to encourage, re-energize, and ask how we can provide support. If the young people who live in the culture are the ones whose voices and actions shape it, you are already meeting many youth needs and creating the type of culture where young people will thrive.

Partnering with Local Organizations

Norms are established through the subtle actions of influential people. The collective mentalities that make up cultures can be beneficial or unhealthy. An insular community with few outside influences—a "bubble," as students love to say—can protect its members or it can harm them. Partnering with vetted outside influences is key to keeping organizations' cultures grounded and healthy.

One school I worked for, for example, developed strong partnerships and consistent communication with outside local organizations through an initiative called the Child Protection Team. As reports of abuse in boarding schools, other private schools, and youth organizations continued to flood news outlets, I was determined to do my due diligence and fully understand my role and responsibility in terms of student-to-student misconduct as well as educator-to-student misconduct. I felt confident in our established protocols, trainings, and prevention programs, but I recognized that our school lacked strong communication with local authorities. When I was hired, there was an acknowledged gap between the school and local law enforcement. It seemed that some historic disagreements and a conflict of personalities in power were interfering with a healthy partnership. Knowing that I could not do my job of protecting the young people in my care effectively without a positive partnership, I sent the following invitation:

Dear Local Law Enforcement, Medical Services, Advocates, and Educators,

At our school, we pride ourselves on providing a safe environment in which students develop academic skills and so much more. Over many years, our school has built policies and processes to prevent, and respond to, the physical abuse, neglect, sexual abuse, and emotional abuse of children. The next step in bettering our practice to best serve our students is the creation of a Child Protection Team. The goal is to gather a group of internal community members and external experts who come together annually and as needed to review our prevention, policies, and practices.

Child Protection Team (CPT)
This team is made up of the following community members:
- *Dean of Community Life*
- *Dean of Students*
- *Assistant Dean of Students*
- *Human Resources Manager*
- *Director of Medical Services*
- *Two teacher volunteers*
- *Four student volunteers*
- *Two Board Members*
- *Local Chapter Representative of the Coalition Against Domestic Violence*
- *Child Advocacy Center Representative*
- *Chief of Police*

This team focuses on reviewing our school in the following areas:
   - ***Prevention**—review the education that students, faculty, and staff are receiving with regard to the prevention of physical abuse, neglect, sexual abuse, and emotional abuse, and make recommendations for future programming and focus.*

• **Practice**—*review incidents in an anonymous fashion to ensure compliance of established procedures.*
• **Policy**—*review policies, complaint procedures, reporting responsibilities, and support systems.*
By solidifying our relationships with local authorities and organizations through the development of this team, we hope to not just meet the standards of child protection and safety, but also be a leader amongst our peer independent schools. We are highly motivated to provide the best possible care and education for our students, and we believe the Child Protection Team will assist us in furthering this mission.

This was the beginning of a complete shift in culture. The invitation opened the door to local organizations that had always wanted to partner with and assist our school but didn't have a way in. For me, sitting around a table with these experts and allowing them to assess my work was terrifying, but what I found was that they were caring, compassionate, and committed professionals, who wanted what I wanted: healthy, happy kids. These were adults who cared deeply about the safety of children, and who had a wealth of experience and knowledge far exceeding mine. Over time, this partnership grew into much more than a way to prevent or address abuse. We at the school learned that we had access to many free preventative programs run by experts in a variety of fields, including substance abuse, sexual assault prevention, suicide prevention, and active shooter response. The local organizations even relied on us to keep them informed of adolescent behavior trends. Through these active partnerships, each party felt like they were gaining something valuable and we all felt strongly that the students were benefiting most of all.

When I recommend partnership, I recommend it far beyond the example I have provided here. I have witnessed summer camps partner with local dentist's offices to provide dental hygiene lessons and tooth cleanings. I have seen schools partner with local law enforcement for bike safety lessons. I witnessed the leaders of a dojo partner with an after-school program to provide self-defense and leadership classes. I attended a business session where local entrepreneurs shared their stories with a mentor/mentee program. And I have seen multiple nonprofit organizations that work to support minority students facilitate trainings for educators, camp counselors, and coaches. These are just a few of the ways I have seen all kinds of adults with different skills and expertise come together to support one another in their work with young people.

The independent school I discuss in the example above had its own culture and set of norms, and the partnership I describe may not be ideal for you and your organization. I encourage you, however, to pop the bubble and allow potential partners in to help assess your program, hold up the mirror, and continue improving and bettering your culture so you can best meet the needs of your young people.

Partnering with Graduates

One of the greatest opportunities to burst the bubble and keep your organization connected to the world is through the young people who once participated in your program—and then grew up! If they had a positive experience and connected with trusted adults, they will no doubt be thrilled to return to your home base and reconnect. I speak here from firsthand experience: I love returning to my schools, camps, ice rinks—anywhere that brings back memories of growth and development. Standing in the space, surrounded by the people who influenced the person you eventually became, is a fulfilling and powerful experience. If a person had a negative experience, however, they'll likely show no desire to return. This is a great measure of the success of your program—do people come back to visit?

One incredibly successful program we hosted at our school, an idea borrowed from the high school I attended, was called Ethics Day. For this special program, we invited a dozen graduates across an array of careers. In my time hosting the event we had pilots, athletic trainers, farm equipment engineers, chefs, school administrators, prison wardens, actors, doctors, environmental advocates, editors, politicians, marketing managers, financial planners, and many others. Senior students had the opportunity to read the biographies of the returning graduates and rank the people they would be most interested in meeting with. We also prepared them ahead of time with a workshop on the importance of networking, handshakes, conversation starters, and other life skills often overlooked in the classroom. It was the perfect opportunity to teach skills and put them into practice immediately.

On the day of the event, the graduates were asked to bring with them an ethical dilemma that they had faced in their current career. Students were divided into groups of about ten and paired with a graduate. The graduate would introduce themselves, learn about the young people at the table, deliver the dilemma (without revealing how they actually handled the situation), and then sit back and observe. The students had to work through a timed protocol, and eventually reach a final decision. This protocol included prompts that helped students define the dilemma, ask clarifying questions, and analyze the issue. They then had to propose actions and evaluate the options using a framework for ethical decision making.

When the group had come to a consensus, or when time had run out, the graduate shared the actions they took following this real-life situation, as well as whether they were satisfied with the actions or regretted their approach, and how they would handle things differently in hindsight. Typically, large sighs, gasps, laughs, and other excited reactions followed when the graduate revealed the real ending of their story. Students and graduates then had to partner to report out to the larger group and share their dilemma and decided approach.

The stories shared and connections made created an invaluable day for all. One graduate said, "I loved the Ethics Day exchange with the students. Most importantly, my wife and I felt like we really connected with a number of them. Please encourage them to reach out to either of us for anything. We were so impressed with them! I'm not sure I would have been diving into a debate on labor laws at eighteen, but they had so many good ideas and thoughts to share." A teacher who hosted one of the graduates commented, "At this event, students are forced to dig into difficult, real-world challenges that they may face in their future. Their comfort zone is pushed and their moral compasses questioned. The best kind of education happened here today, and it happened while they connected with relatable adults." I share this as an example of a way to positively reconnect with graduates because the value it brings to the current young people in your care is immediate. Graduates of your program can return to speak to large groups, as often happens, but realize that there are other options for including and engaging graduates that really benefit current students.

Turn Your Graduates into Trusted Adults

Ideas for engaging graduates of your youth-serving organization:

- Create a mentor/mentee program and connect graduates one on one with your current youth.
- Begin a shadow day, or a go-to-work-with-a-graduate day, where teens from your organization can learn from your graduates in a real-world setting.

- Invite graduates back for a camp or campus cleanup day to help out with current students or campers, creating a bond through good ol'-fashioned hard work.
- Survey your graduates one, five, and ten years after they complete your program about how their experience with your organization influenced their choices, actions, and success. Ask directly how your organization could have better met their needs as a young person, and solicit their advice to current young people in your organization.
- Ask them how they want to stay connected and how they want to support the youth currently in your program.

The types of graduates you choose to invite back, and those your organization celebrates, tell a story to the current youth in your care about what matters. Do you celebrate the wealthy grads? The ones committed to taking environmental action? The alumni paying it forward and serving others? The athletes? The artists? The musicians? As important as the words that plaster your hallways is the message you send your youth about who gets celebrated. What you celebrate, you endorse. A main ingredient in your organization's cultural soil is how it defines and advertises the term *success*. Use your maintained connections with graduates of your program as an opportunity to define, demonstrate, and strengthen your values, mission, and culture.

Partnering with Parents

One partnership we haven't yet jumped into fully is among the most important—our partnership with the parents and guardians of the young people we work with. When I started writing this book, I asked myself: After reading about all the cases of abuse, why should parents and guardians still hand their children off to coaches, teachers, priests, band directors, and other adults who might harm them? I thought about the number of times I hand my own son over to adults I don't know well. I thought about the number of times that I, as a child, was handed over to adults my parents didn't really know. It starts when kids are still in diapers, whether the adult is an occasional babysitter or a regular worker at day care and it continues all through the child's growing-up years, as we turn to one adult after another to help us fill the gaps.

The reason we keep putting our children in the care of other adults is because the benefits outweigh the risk. I see the proposition as similar to riding in an airplane. Planes can indeed crash, but the likelihood is actually very small. When I step onboard an aircraft I am putting my life in the hands of an adult I don't know, and I expect them to be professional and to take their responsibility seriously. The parenting partnership with trusted adults is similar. The potential that an adult will harm a child exists, and there is no denying that fact; however, the adults in your community have so much to offer your child that you would effectively shrink your child's world if you were to avoid allowing them to form relationships with other adults.

But the relationship with another trusted adult is not the only benefit your child will take away from time spent with grown-ups. *Child Trends* reported that "those [children] who have a caring adult outside the home are more likely to talk with their parents about 'things that really matter.'" Having trusted adults outside the family actually strengthens the relationships inside the family.

At the beginning of each school year, a colleague of mine said to parents who were dropping their kids off at boarding school for the first time: "*You* are the expert on *your adolescent* please trust that we are the experts on *adolescents.*" I believe this helped set a trustful tone: he was telling them, in essence, that we, as the soon-to-be trusted adults, wholeheartedly respected their years of experience as a parent of this child, and they should respect our years of collective experience educating and caring for all kinds of children. He would follow up by saying, "Adolescents say a lot of things. We encourage you to only believe 50 percent of what they say about us. If you do this, we will return the favor, and only believe 50 percent of what they say about you." This always got a rousing laugh and perfectly encapsulated his deep understanding and appreciation for adolescents and all that comes with raising them.

The conversation regarding parent partnering has been ongoing for many years. Sara Lawrence-Lightfoot, an education professor at Harvard University and an expert on this topic, has been writing on the relationships between family and school since 1978. She states in her book *The Essential Conversation: What Parents and Teachers Can Learn from Each Other* that "Productive collaborations between family and school demand that parents and teachers recognize the critical importance of each other's participation in the life of the child. This mutuality of knowledge, understanding, and empathy comes not only with a recognition of the child as the central purpose for the collaboration but also with a recognition of the need to maintain roles and relationships with children that are comprehensive, dynamic, and differentiated." Some families and schools perform this delineation of roles and understanding of critical impact magically. Others struggle. It was the mother of one of my students who taught me how much easier this relationship can be navigated if everyone is upfront with expectations.

With five daughters ranging from middle school to college age, this mother had seen many versions of trusted adults through her children's experiences. Growing up with multiple grounded, knowledgeable, and trusted adults herself, and owing much of her success to their support, she knew it was a priority to surround her girls with the same. She witnessed the good and bad in teachers, swim coaches, nannies, employers, dorm parents, and running coaches. She provided me with a short list of questions that parents can ask themselves (and others, if necessary) as they encourage their kids to form relationships with other adults, while balancing the desire to stay out of the way with the need to ensure the child's health and safety. She and her husband ask themselves the following questions regularly:

- Is this adult building my child's self-esteem?
- What is motivating this adult to work with young people?
- Are they willing to have a relationship and engage with us as parents?

She also has what she calls a "cause for pause" moment. If she and her husband pause when answering the questions above, they know that there is a potential concern that needs to be addressed. She will not hesitate to contact the adult and ask the questions directly.

As a recipient of one of these e-mails, I found this parent's approach helpful and encouraging. I served as a dorm parent and advisor for one of her daughters. The e-mail began, "I have a few questions I would like to ask you as a trusted adult in my daughter's life." Had I not been doing my job appropriately, I imagine this e-mail would have caused me some anxiety (and rightfully so), but I was proud that my work with her daughter was so effective that the girl was reporting to her parents that she trusted me.

Most often, parents want strong partnerships with the schools and programs their kids are involved in. After all, parents and other trusted adults have the best interest of the child in mind. At times, however, conflict arises when a parent's expectations surpass the abilities of the child or the organization to meet those expectations. Dealing with unhappy parents is difficult. Being honest from the beginning, keeping communication open, and acting professionally can prevent a situation from getting to a point that the actions and reactions of the adults pull the focus away from what is best for the child. When conflicts are inevitable, rely on organization policies and leaders. Listen, take responsibility, and remind parents that a healthy and cooperative partnership between them and other trusted adults in their child's life is always what is best for the young person.

In a chapter titled "The Handshake Between Families and Schools," in the book *Letters to a Young Education Reformer,* Frederick Hess says: "When asking parents to clasp hands with educators, things like support, expectations, and peer pressure can make a huge difference. Reformers need to think not just about how schools and teachers can do better but also about what it means for parents to do better. In both cases, change is partly a matter of appreciation and problem solving—and partly a matter of tough love. This isn't an either-or. Everyone needs to step up." I appreciate Hess's approach to the partnership between trusted adults and parents or guardians—everyone can always do better.

Building and maintaining a positive culture and productive partnerships is a slow and incremental process. Daily attention and thoughtful action must be given to creating healthy soil and solid ground for the good work to occur. A simple bulletin board test can gauge the culture of your organization—walk around the space where your organization does its work and write down every large word you see on a bulletin board, poster, or the walls. Sit with your team and ask: Is this who we are? And, more importantly, is this who we want to be? If we say it, we will do it, and we will become it. Then have someone from the outside come in and do the same, and ask them to tell you what they see. Fresh eyes reveal to us messages we may be unintentionally sending to our constituents, but that we can't see because we are so close to those messages.

We also need to accept that we may not be all for everyone. We may not have the best trusted adults in our ranks for a specific child. We may not be able to teach or deliver the services most needed. Owning this reality and partnering with outside organizations can solve this problem and provide a more well-rounded experience and education for the children in your care. Whether these partners are law enforcement, other local organizations, graduates, or parents, there is much that children can gain by having a healthy and positive team of adults in their corner.

CHAPTER 11

Opening the Door
to Critical Conversations:
Why We Need a Curriculum

Earlier in the book, I quoted a training participant, Mrs. O'Neill, who reminded us that "Algebra is the avenue, not the destination." There is a caveat to the statement, however: it is true if, and only if, the organization, as a whole, has chosen to adopt a culture that believes the destination is growing well-rounded, educated, confident young people who are prepared to take care of themselves and believe in the importance of caring for others.

Residential curriculum, advisory curriculum, health and wellness class, social-emotional development, leadership class—call the program what you will, every school (and many organizations), have a bucket into which we pour everything we need to teach young people that falls outside the academic curriculum. The programs have different catchy names, like Leap, Peaks, Compass, Launch, Choices, Step Up, and Jump, but they all aim to do the same job of talking with and teaching students about important life skills, wellness practices, and social-emotional proficiencies that are absent from the traditional classroom.

The effort isn't always centered around a formal program, however, nor does it always have a formal name. If a group of educators and adult influencers in an organization believe that their sports practices, music rehearsals, and after-school programs provide students with opportunities for life skills education, then they subtly turn their fields, theaters, and rehearsal rooms into effective life skills classrooms. I applaud soccer coaches and theater directors who believe that, as important as the time spent dribbling the ball or rehearsing lines may be, the time spent teaching discipline, honesty, time management, perseverance, and empathy is just as critical. An already established passion or interest, such as theater or soccer, is even better than algebra as an avenue for real-world life skills learning.

There are many ways organizations can more intentionally weave life skills, social-emotional development, and wellness practices into their existing programs. In this chapter, we will explore the reasons organizations should commit their time, resources and focus to developing life skills and social-emotional development programs, including those that focus on prevention of risk, more influential response to infractions, and the opportunity for deeper connections with trusted adults. We will also discuss strategies for getting your entire team on board with viewing themselves as life skills educators.

Prevention

When I ask groups of educators to finish the sentence, "The best trusted adults . . ." I rarely hear the response ". . . facilitate life skills curricula." I recognize the delivery of life skills education isn't always top of mind. But life skills lessons and wellness workshops, whether formal or informal, that deliver an agreed-upon set of skills, values, and preventative information not only passes critical knowledge on to students but also opens the door to other conversations a young person may need to have. An adult opening the door to a conversation about self-care, consent, suicide, substance use and abuse, sex, or stress is an adult opening a door to a conversation about anything. The trust built between an adult and a young person offers an incredible opportunity for the young person to learn important life skills, and the relationship alone can shield them from risk.

In Dr. Frances Jensen's book *The Teenage Brain*, she writes:

> You have to be proactive. You have to stuff their minds with real stories, real consequences, and then you have to do it again— over dinner, after soccer practice, before music lessons, and, yes, even when they complain they've heard it all before. You have to remind them: These things can happen anytime, and there are many different situations that can get them into trouble, and that can end badly.

Jensen goes on to express the importance of young people having the opportunity to unpack the events that are happening around them and process their experiences with a trusted adult. Young people bear witness to the daily actions of their peers— getting in trouble at school, making risky choices and getting away with it, hurting the feelings of others, and hurting themselves. Their observations can confuse them at a time when they are calibrating their own inner-values compass; if they have a space to unpack, process, and seek to understand with a trusted adult, the muddy waters of middle and high school can be made a little clearer, and the pieces of mirror on their disco ball can come together to make a larger picture that makes a little more sense.

Jensen also makes the case for repetition, as the adolescent frontal lobe is on a delay, which means not only is decision making under development but memory is basically on hold. We think that if we have let them know once that we are open to any and all conversations, that should be enough. But that's like brushing your teeth once a month and figuring all is good. It's kind of like my attitude toward gym attendance—the benefits of one hard workout should last at least a couple of weeks, right? Instead, think of life skills and conversational work with young people as more like sleep—it has to be a regular part of your days. Continually building trust and having proactive conversations is as important for our self-care as daily hygiene habits. It is imperative that we remind young people that we are trusted adults, and that we open the door to conversations as often as possible.

Creating an informal space—I think of it as a metaphorical kitchen table—within your program is highly effective for these conversations. In an article titled "Reclaiming the Family Table: Mealtimes and Child Health and Wellbeing," published in *Social Policy Report*, authors Barbara Fiese and Marlene Schwartz state that "the outcomes associated with mealtimes are precisely those outcomes of considerable interest to developmental scientists: risk reduction, achievement of developmental milestones (i.e., language development), and overall heath." Knowing the effectiveness of conversations held around the kitchen table, the question becomes, how do we create spaces like this in our organizations and programs?

In graduate school, I studied educational theater. The tactics I learned in this course of study helped me understand how effective learning is when it is brought to life. Through activities, reflection, sharing, and videos, we can make the content we want to transmit relevant and impactful, and it can all be done at the metaphorical kitchen table. Here are some tips for facilitating conversations about important life skills in a group setting:

1. Recognize that there is no "grade" in these conversations, and therefore there is no "teacher." An honest dialogue and sharing of knowledge must be the motivator. Your role is as a facilitator.
2. Convey the importance of these conversations. Because we have trained young people to be motivated by grades and cumulative GPA, you may find it difficult to convince young people that these conversations are worthwhile. Some will feel, "If I don't get a grade, it doesn't matter." Your job as a facilitator is to make these topics matter by bringing them alive through story and real-world events.
3. Be fully present for the conversation. Ask that all technology be put away—including yours.
4. Work on a set of group agreements. Example: Step up, step back (if you talk often, take a step back; if you haven't shared, take a step up). Ask your group what other agreements are important for everyone to feel safe and heard in the conversation.
5. Acknowledge the right to "pass." Recognize that everyone comes to the table with a different history, a different understanding of the topic, a different family culture, and a different willingness to approach difficult topics. If a young person wants to pass (not share) or step out of the room, always allow this. If you are in a school setting, it is best that you direct them to a guidance counselor or nurse. If that is not an option, you should leave your group to check in with the student.
6. Keep track of squirrels. Stay focused on the topic at hand but keep track of side issues that come up and are worth exploring. When the conversation takes a turn away from the focus, I always say, "Squirrel!" as something has pulled our attention, just like my dogs are distracted by a squirrel on the trail. Make a list of squirrels, and revisit them after the main conversation has concluded.

7. Remind your young people that you are a mandated reporter. Always let them know that if you are made aware of neglect or abuse, you are required by law to seek the support of experts. Let them know that you want this conversation to be as open and honest as possible, but you also want them to be aware of your obligations.

8. If things are just not clicking that day, get up and move, play a game, do an icebreaker, tell a story, or ask them: If you were to create a workshop on this topic for your age group, what would you do? This always enlivens the conversation!

9. Always, always model the behavior you want young people to follow. Practice what you preach. They are always watching.

10. Last, make it yours! Believe in what you are offering, bring energy to it, and deliver it in the way that feels best to you.

A focus on raising competent, informed, and prepared adults with an understanding of what they need to know to embrace their lives fully, rather than a singular focus on bringing home championships and ultrahigh SAT scores, sends a strong message about the organization's culture and the types of relationships it promotes. And championship coaches and AP teachers come to recognize the importance of opening the door to conversations when their students show up far more focused and present to pursue greatness after being given a place to process their reality. These important conversations provide relief—they validate young people's thoughts and confusion surrounding relationships, choices, identity, substance use and abuse, technology, and so on. They also prevent young people from making the risky choices they might have made if they did not have the information they needed or a safe place to unpack their thoughts and feelings.

Response

I have always believed in the benefit of proactive conversations with young people to keep them safe and out of trouble; when students made risky choices that violated an organizational rule, my general feeling was that our preventative work had failed. It was not until eight years into my career in independent schools that I got a front-row seat to the importance of an intentional life skills curriculum on the reactive side of a poor choice, even though we had failed to prevent it. My approach to discipline has always been to have a conversation and get to the root of the issue. I can certainly hand out punishments like detentions and work detail, but these slaps on the wrist do little on their own to adjust behavior. Behind an adolescent's choice to break the rules is often anxiety, misinformation, conflict, a substance problem, or a misled desire to fill a youth need. Conversations and time together typically get us to a better understanding of choices and behavior, and help us set up consequences and support that make the most sense for the particular child and situation.

The instance for which I had a front-row seat followed two high school juniors getting very drunk at a school event. On the night of the event, they were caught in the act by another teacher and taken to the health center. Their parents were informed, medical needs were taken care of, and they were scheduled to meet with me the next day. The first young man came into my office and sat down, his head hanging in shame and embarrassment. We made small talk while I waited for his advisor to join us. This advisor was a very good advisor, and I knew from general observations that he was a trusted adult for this young man. What I hadn't realized was that they hadn't spoken about the incident yet. Here is how the encounter went, once the advisor entered my office.

Student: "I know . . . I know. . . before you say anything, I know."
Advisor: "What do you know?"
Student: "I know that last week in advisory we had a group conversation about substance abuse. And I shared that I have watched my dad ruin his life and our family through alcoholism. And I never want that to happen to me or anyone else I know. I told you I hate alcohol for that reason. Never did I think less than a week later I would be sitting here with the two of you, in trouble for this. I'm a moron."

At this point, I just sat back and let the work happen in front of me. This adult had earned the trust and respect of this young man through open and honest dialogue about tough topics. And those hard conversations were paying off in the here and now. The advisor's work may not have prevented this risky choice, but it had planted a seed that was going to make this conversation far more effective than anything I could do.

Advisor: "I don't think you're a moron, although I think you did something moronic."
Student: "I know. I just said yes when I should have said no. It happened so fast. He offered it, I said yes, I just said yes. And I have no idea why I didn't say no. It's not like I felt pressure. I don't think. I don't know. I mean, I know. I just don't know."
Advisor: "Let's dig in on that. You said yes when you should have said no. Keep talking that out. Why do you think you should have said no?"
Student: "I am asking a lot of my body right now with swimming, and I have been super smart about eating and sleeping, and I should have said no because vodka is not going to help me be a better swimmer. I also know it was against the rules, and I don't want to get kicked out of school or kicked off the swim team. I want to be a leader next year. There are a lot of reasons I should have said no."

Advisor: "Those are important reasons. Thanks for sharing. Now . . . where were those reasons hidden in your head when you said yes?"

The dialogue went back and forth like this for half an hour, and I felt so lucky to be a witness. By the end of our time, I knew it was not the end of theirs, and that this kitchen table conversation would continue far beyond my office. We agreed to specific school consequences, and the student agreed to keep talking to his advisor and parents about his decision making.

At the end of this meeting, I felt like a champion. Like we had finally completed our build of a culture with a focus on the growth and development of young people. Like my team got it. In the moments to come, however, I was quickly brought back to reality.

The next junior boy and his advisor entered my office and sat down. Because the last conversation surrounding the advisory curriculum on substance use had gone so well, I decided to start there.

Me: "Let's begin by talking about the substance use curriculum from last week's advisory period."
Student: "Uhhhhhh . . . I don't think we did that."
Advisor: [*looking at me sheepishly*]
Me: "Okay . . . well, then . . . why don't you share with me what happened last night?"
Student: "Pretty sure you already know. I drank alcohol and got caught. What is my punishment?"

My bubble was burst. Because of the first advisor's commitment to proactive conversations about a real-life topic, we were able to get somewhere educational in a reactive matter. We could talk about human behavior and applicable life skills, focusing on growth and preparation for adulthood. In the second scenario, the emphasis was on discipline and consequence. The conversation was about the rule, instead of about why the rule was enforced—for the health, happiness, safety, and success of the students.

Overall, I believe that proactive conversations help prevent adolescents from making risky choices, but where they fail to prevent, they assist us in responding.

Pushback

In loco parentis, a Latin phrase tossed around at schools and other youth organizations, describes the role an educator or the organization has in caring for a student in place of their parent. This phrase takes on deeper meaning for boarding schools and overnight programs such as camps and study-abroad programs, where young people are away from home for an extended period. Even at day schools, however, teachers often spend more hours per day with a child than their own parents do. Isn't it, then, our duty and responsibility to participate in these important conversations about wellness and life skills? Still, I receive pushback from educators who do not believe it is their job or responsibility to go anywhere near the topics of sex, suicide, or substances, to name a few! Here are common pushback statements, and my answers:

> **Comment:** Is this content really relevant and necessary?
> **Reply:** We can certainly make an effort to create a curriculum that is relevant for our students by surveying them on the climate of our culture as well as by using national youth risk and behavior surveys to inform our topics. Including students as we develop the conversation topics and curriculum is incredibly effective. I want to remind you, too, that the content isn't always what is most important—you, the trusted adult, opening the door to conversation is key.

Comment: We don't have enough time.
Reply: You're right. The administrators and leaders of this organization need to make this curriculum a priority and make time for it. You are an influencer of their decisions. If you believe these life skills are important to kids, voice that. If you spend the time with your young people on this work, I promise they will be more focused, attentive, accessible, and productive in the tasks you need them to complete.

Comment: It's not my job to have these conversations.
Reply: I would argue that it is your most important job. You have chosen work that involves young people. Raising strong, confident, and informed young people is a big—and possibly the biggest—part of this job.

Comment: I'm not trained for this.
Reply: We are not asking you to be an expert in anything; that's what Google is for. Your role is to facilitate a conversation, to provide an open and safe space in which you and the young people in your care can discuss important topics. You will need to express your vulnerability, admit your limits, learn along with your students, and process together.

Then I share this story: At a school where I worked, part of my role was to develop a life skills curriculum and train our advisors to deliver it. I was met with resistance by a few faculty members who loved to use statements like those above, and one who was particularly adamant that she not be asked to participate. She was a thirty-year veteran faculty member, a fantastic teacher, and a revered coach, and she was highly respected by her students. In one of the faculty trainings I was leading, she stood up and asked to say something about the life skills conversations. Knowing that she was one of the lead resistors when it came to these conversations, I was nervous. Here is what she shared:

For the last year, when Brook has sent us this curriculum, I have deleted her e-mails. I did not think it was relevant or necessary. Our kids are good kids who are making good choices. And I just don't like talking about drugs, sex, alcohol, anxiety, et cetera—it makes me uncomfortable—I would rather talk about their grades. A few months ago, my nephew died of an overdose. He was a top student, a ski racer, he was attending a good college, and he was the last person on the planet that I would believe would die of an overdose. This has shaken me, and makes me worry about our students.

Since this tragedy, I have reevaluated my role in my students' lives. What can I do to make sure this doesn't happen to someone else? I dug the "Substance Use and Abuse" lesson plan out of my virtual trash bin and have been delivering every bit of our advisory curriculum since then. The reaction of my group has shocked me. They seem quiet in our time together, but almost every single one of them has circled back around to chat with me at some point about the discussion. They all have a story connected to each of the topics we tackle. Some of them are even coming back to me to share things that are not related to the content of the lesson. I feel as though I opened one door to having one tough conversation, and it has blown open the doors to entirely different and more meaningful relationships with my advisees. I thought that as I aged, my students were going to pull away as my experiences were less relatable, but the conversations through this curriculum have connected us and helped me get to know my advisees, and let them get to know me, better than ever.

This teacher's story is powerful because it is honest. It is a reminder that the life skills conversations are much more than a curriculum. They are a gateway to authentic discussion and stronger relationships between adults and young people.

By opening these conversations with adolescents, adults establish themselves as reliable and significant role models in their students' lives. The importance of this work cannot be overstated. A commitment to wellness, risk prevention, and helping youth develop strong relationships with trusted adults decreases disciplinary issues, makes for meaningful growth when rules are broken, and increases engagement and healthy choices. It encourages leadership and bystander intervention, and will fill your organizations with more attentive and accessible students, athletes, artists, and community members.

C'MON: Teaching Life Skills

When I prepare a life skills or wellness program for young people, I work it through a model I developed called C'MON: Curriculum, Model, Obstacle, Now What? Here is how it works:

Curriculum: What is it we are trying to teach?
Let's work through the model with two examples: 1. Leadership skills, including communication and collaboration 2. Sexual consent education.

Model: Do I have the right staff with the right training and tools in place to model what we are teaching?

If we are teaching leadership, communication, and collaboration, we'd better have a staff that can lead, communicate, and collaborate. If we are teaching sexual consent education, we need a staff that respects the choices of those around them, and shows how to ask for and give consent in all daily interactions.

Obstacle: How can we challenge what we have taught?

Example: At Girls' Leadership Camp, we have campers build picnic tables, climb mountains, camp out, and do other activities that challenge the leadership skills we are teaching. With a sexual consent education curriculum, it would be important to work through scenarios and discuss how what we learned would play out in each. Scenarios need to reiterate the teachings of consent being freely given, reversible, informed, enthusiastic, and specific—whether the discussion is about sex or any other actions that might impact another person.

Now What?: How are the skills relevant to life beyond the space where they were taught?

Example: At GLC, we have something called a Leader Log, where written exercises ask the girls to reflect, push their thinking, and document the lessons that are most important to them and how these lessons are relevant in their schools and homes. In terms of sexual consent education, it would be important to debrief the conversation by asking where and when this type of information is relevant in the young people's lives, and who else needs to hear it.

The C'MON model helps keep the programs I design relevant and meaningful. It also gives me a framework for discussing with our staff what we, as an organization, are doing and why. This approach has proven valuable in gaining the full buy-in of students because it keeps the focus on teaching, modeling, and keeping the topic and skills relevant to life beyond our metaphorical kitchen table.

Through a commitment to teaching life skills, you will naturally develop a kitchen table culture where young people yearn for these moments, where they can gather in small groups with an adult they trust to talk about life's confusing and compelling challenges. I remember moments like this from my high school experience vividly. Some of my greatest memories revolve around a few of my friends and a trusted adult sitting in a circle, eating donuts and processing the events of the week. When working with youth, plan for these moments to be both powerful and worth your time. If you have been tasked to teach archery, plan to also teach mindfulness. If you have been tasked with running an outdoor program, plan to also discuss personal hygiene. If your job description says teacher of algebra, plan to teach grit and resilience. You will get more from your young people by giving more, expanding beyond your specific discipline to teach valuable life skills they'll need for the long haul.

CHAPTER 12

Breaking the Silence and Embracing a Feedback Loop

When I facilitate adult trainings, I put the F word up on the screen. Feedback, that is. I then ask everyone to write down six words that come to mind when they first hear the F word. I invite them to raise their hands if their words were generally positive (examples: improvement, growth, educational, care). About half of the room raises their hands.

Then I ask for a show of hands from those whose words were generally negative (examples: aggressive, mean, disconnected, harsh). The other half of the room raises their hands. Then I invite the group to raise their hands if, when they reflected on the word feedback, they immediately thought about *giving* feedback to the students/athletes they work with. Every time I do this, I see nearly the same raised hands of those who reported a *positive* association with the word feedback. Finally, I invite participants to raise their hands if, when they reflected on the word feedback, they immediately thought about *receiving* feedback from a supervisor or manager. Almost exactly the same hands go up as those who reported a *negative* association with the word feedback. These trainings lead me to believe that, generally, we have a far better experience giving feedback than receiving it.

Feedback can have a negative impact on an organization's culture if it is not delivered well, but it's invaluable when handled the right way. Schools and youth organizations that promote free-flowing, desired, and eagerly received feedback have people who are healthier, happier, and more engaged. When colleagues are accountable, the whole team feels safer and better equipped to create a healthy culture for youth.

Resistance to Feedback

Before we dive into how to give and receive feedback, and its significance for maintaining a healthy culture, let's understand what gets in the way of a well-meaning, ongoing feedback system in most organizations. Kim Malone, in her book *Radical Candor: Be a Kickass Boss Without Losing Your Humanity,* says, "When bosses are too invested in everyone getting along they also fail to encourage the people on their team to criticize one another for fear of sowing discord. They create the kind of work environment where being 'nice' is prioritized at the expense of critiquing and therefore improving actual performance." This type of "nice" environment unfortunately leads to cultures where unhealthy, illegal, and harmful acts occur year after year without anyone breaking the silence and questioning the behaviors. People avoid confrontation because it is uncomfortable.

I find it fascinating that we adults think so hard about the model of feedback we will use to grade and comment on the work and performance of the young people in our lives, but we do not spend the same amount of time thinking through the best ways to provide feedback to one another. Our natural reactions are to ignore, complain about, or report our colleagues.

There is a growing resistance to feedback, and this arises out of previous negative experiences, technology advances, and competitive cultures. I see in my students and my colleagues, and often in myself, a desire for approval and a pat on the back rather than criticism or honest feedback. Because we are consistently receiving messages that we are inadequate—through social media and through outlets trying to sell us products to make up for our shortcomings—we often turn to (in person or electronically) our closest supports, who will tell us whatever we need to hear to feel like we are enough. Competition, technology, and negative experiences have moved us from a place of desiring honest feedback for the purposes of improvement to one where we want soothing reassurance, even if what we are hearing is not offering us opportunity for growth.

In a culture where instant gratification is the norm, we become convinced that if we don't get what we want right now from this person, we can, and should, seek it somewhere else. This tendency, along with inconsistent (or even nonexistent) evaluation and feedback systems in our workplaces and relationships, leaves us feeling shocked and under personal attack when we do receive feedback. Too often, we are underprepared and ill equipped to receive and put into practice any advice for better performance. Malone also notes that, "The way you ask for criticism and react when you get it goes a long way toward building trust—or destroying it," reinforcing the impact that giving and receiving feedback can play in building relationships and culture.

Of course, no one wants to hear their shortcomings, but isn't there a way to structure feedback so that your team craves the support and advice they need to thrive? After a training I facilitated with a group of teachers on the topic of giving and receiving feedback, one experienced teacher came up to me afterward and told me the following:

This is important work you are doing. I wish we had done a training like this in my early years. When I first started as a twenty-three-year-old teacher—before laptops, cell phones, e-mail, yes, I am old—we were simply told to speak up and hold our colleagues accountable. No one told us where or how. So, I used the same system we used to write up the students. I filled out a little yellow slip, and I put it in the principal's mailbox. I wrote my colleagues up for everything—leaving their lunch in the fridge too long, talking loudly in the hallway, being out of dress code—I mean, everything! I look back now and just shake my head at myself. Eventually, I started getting the slips back in my mailbox. In red pen, the principal had written "These sound like issues that you are capable of handling, and my attention and expertise can be better used elsewhere." Of course, I should have been addressing my grievances to my colleagues myself! But I had no tools for, or practice, doing it.

Take a group of grown people who are committed in different ways, and with different skills and talents, to the same cause—preparing adolescents to become capable adults—and put them in one room, then ask them to design a school. These adults may all have the same goal in raising adolescents to become independent and responsible, but not all will agree on the path to get there. In the schools and groups I work with regularly, the same conflicts among the adults come up again and again. These conflicts almost always arise over issues of time, resources, effort, attention, and consistency.

I do not have magical answers for creating more time and resources. I wish I did! I do, however, have a reliable way to train colleagues to give and receive feedback. The Ouch-Thank You Approach will influence the way colleagues hold one another accountable for maximum effort, attention to responsibilities, and consistency in their work.

This approach shapes the way we receive feedback; we agree to simply say, "Ouch, thank you" and sit with what we have heard until we are prepared to thoughtfully respond or act. The key to this approach is that it is agreed upon by the team before any conflict arises. By deciding together how we, as a team, will give feedback, and how we, as a team, will receive feedback, we set ourselves up to build more trust and better boundaries, break the silence around improper or abusive behavior, and create a healthy and safe culture that supports the adults and the kids. This approach is the closest thing to a magic wand we will find!

Embracing Feedback

Three stories are emblematic of my understanding of feedback, and these experiences helped me gather my thoughts on the topic and create the Ouch-Thank You Approach for individuals and organizations to put into practice. These stories involve a Canadian massage therapist, a Fitbit, and my maid of honor. Yes, I'm serious.

Truth

It was December of my sixth year working in education, and I had made it halfway through my toughest school year yet. I felt beat up and exhausted. I had not been taking care of myself physically or emotionally because I had been busy doing that for others, and quite simply I did not make self-care a priority.

My husband and I had gone to my hometown in Canada to celebrate Christmas with family, and on our way back my husband treated me to a night in Niagara Falls and, most importantly, a professional massage! I walked into the beautiful spa and was sent to my appointment room with a robe. I awkwardly undressed, got under the sheet, and waited for the knock. A strong-looking massage therapist walked in, and for unknown reasons I started telling her all the reasons I deserved to be spoiling myself with an hour-long massage: "As you will soon see, I have so many knots in my back. I'm really tight. I work really hard. It's been a tough year. I'm super stressed. I'm probably overdoing it, but I'm pretty important. I work really hard. Did I tell you how stressed I am?"

And then, like a freight train, she hit me with a hard truth right between the eyes. Softly and directly, she said, "Actually, knots and tightness aren't caused by stress or working hard, they are caused by lack of hydration, poor posture, being overweight, and overall unhealthy living." My response: "Ouch. Thank you." *Ouch* because her words stung—and they stung bad. And *thank you* because this stranger, this very strong and direct stranger, had just given me a much-needed mind-set alignment (along with the back alignment).

Timeliness

I used to be among the majority of people who wake up in the morning thinking, "I didn't get enough sleep last night." Whether I really did or didn't, I began every day with this phrase. Looking back, I realize that this was the most incredible disclaimer a person could use. If I had a horrible day at work, epically screwed up, and never wanted to go back, I could go home and say, "Because I didn't get enough sleep last night, I had a terrible day." The blame game was easy. If I had the most fantastic day, achieving more than humanly possible and receiving praise and compliments all around, I could go home and say, "Despite not getting enough sleep last night, I crushed it today!" Starting with a deficit made my efforts even more heroic.

It was a great setup, until my husband called me on it. Concerned about my self-reported lack of sleep, he got me a Fitbit for my birthday so I could track my sleep. Worst gift ever! Wouldn't you know, my first night wearing it that little device reported I had gotten eight hours and nine minutes of sleep. Not believing the results, I still claimed not to have had enough sleep, and I tested it again. Eight hours, twelve minutes. Convincing myself the tracker was broken, I traded Fitbits with my husband the next night—eight hours, six minutes. There was no denying it. I'm a great sleeper. No excuses. No disclaimers. No heroic feats. It was a mind-set problem, not a sleep problem. I would not have been called to the carpet on this if not for immediate feedback from the Fitbit. The timeliness of the feedback means no wiggle room and no rewriting of the truth.

And the feedback didn't stop with sleep. Now, when I get home from work believing that I must have walked 10,000 steps with all the running around I did, I can see that the tracker says 4,567 steps. My response is "Ouch. Thank you." And I hit the track to get in the rest of my daily exercise. Although immediate feedback in this scenario is helpful, it's not always possible at work and in life. What is always possible, however, is a consideration of the timeliness, predictability, and regularity with which you deliver feedback to someone else. Considering the other person's schedule, asking them if it is a good time, and creating an ongoing dialogue sets the person up to truly hear your feedback. If it is truthful feedback being shared for the purposes of improvement, then it must be delivered when the other party is best able to receive it, not when you decide to get it off your chest.

Trust
It was my wedding day. For most people, this would be an exciting and happy time—finally, the big day was here! For me, not so much. I love my husband, and I absolutely wanted to marry him. As an attention junkie, you would think I'd love to have everyone's eyes on me. But, no. I was an ice hockey goalie, so I was used to people staring at me from beyond the glass as I stood in head-to-toe gear looking like the Michelin Man, not close up in a gown and makeup!

Like a good bride, I bit my tongue and did what my mom told me to do. I spent the whole morning at the salon while all my relatives and friends hung out by the pool. Torture. When I finally walked out of the salon, wearing a tiara and feeling like Kate Middleton, I ran into my maid of honor, who happened to be my little sister. Expecting her to tear up and say, "Wow . . . just wow . . ." I was taken aback when instead she said, "Ummmmm . . . why do you look like Ursula from *The Little Mermaid*?" Ouch. Thank you. I think?!

She turned me around, walked me back into the salon, and helped them make me look like me again. In this moment, I could not have taken feedback that direct from anyone but my sister, with whom I have been building a trusting relationship for more than twenty years. While this may seem like a low-stakes example, if you have ever been a bride you can attest to the stress-inducing environment of the bride's quarters on the day of a wedding. There are some things that some people can tell me that others can't. This doesn't have to do with the person's likeability, or credentials, or delivery—it has everything to do with trust.

There it is. Everything I know about feedback comes from these three stories. If the feedback that is given is the truth, is delivered in a time-sensitive way, and comes from a trusted source it should elicit the response, "Ouch. Thank you." *Ouch* for the sting, because the truth is sometimes painful, and *thank you* because someone cares enough to give you their honest opinion. Whether you are talking with a spouse, colleague, student, or camper, this approach will help you deliver feedback so the other can hear it, and receive feedback in a way that allows you to accept and apply it.

Practicing Feedback

This Ouch-Thank You Approach to feedback has bettered my parenting, coaching, teaching, friendships, and also my marriage. So often, when we are given feedback, we have an intrinsic response to defend, excuse, or discredit it.

Here is a recent personal example: My husband said, "Brook, you keep leaving hair in the drain, do you think you can clean it out each time you shower?"

What do you think I wanted to say in this moment? If you have a spouse or a roommate, you know. I desperately wanted to bark back, "Oh yeah? Well your beard trimmings are all over the sink, you left a dirty dish downstairs, you still haven't taken the trash out, there are toenail clippings on the bedside table, and the dinner you cooked last night sucked!"

Did I say that? Nope. Not anymore!

Instead, I said, "Ouch. Thank you." Then I cleaned the hair out of the drain. I needed to hear that. It's gross, and I should be responsible for cleaning up after myself. And, when the time was right, I addressed the issue of the beard trimmings. Guess what he said? "Ouch. Thank you." And then he began cleaning up after trimming his beard.

When the scenario is a little more serious than hair in the drain, here are some effective conversation starters you can rely on when providing feedback colleague to colleague:

My **truth**, and what I am observing is this . . .
The reason for my **timing** with this feedback is . . .
I hope that you can **trust** I brought this to you because . . .

Using the Ouch-Thank You Approach, I have worked with groups to create agreed-upon feedback contracts that they can fall back on in their workplaces and in their work with youth. Recently, a group of teachers I was working with came up with and agreed to the following:

> I, as a member of this team, will *give* feedback in the following way: *Often, timely, positively, objectively, face to face, privately, providing examples.*
> I, as a member of this this team, will *receive* feedback in the following way:
> *Calmly, asking questions, go back to that person, reflect for twenty-four hours, practice "Ouch-Thank You."*

They then made posters and plastered their walls with this visible reminder of the agreement they had made. Following these agreements and relying on the script, we walked through the following scenarios. Because I am all about practice.

1. The teacher next door to your classroom consistently lets class out five minutes early. Your students beg you to get out early too. The students from the other class walk by your door, wave in the window, and cause a distraction. It has become really disruptive to productivity at the end of your class each day. How might you provide feedback to this colleague?
2. You notice a teacher and a student spending a lot of time together. The faculty member does not seem to be doing what they can to keep their meetings "observable and interruptible," which is school policy. You are worried this faculty member has become too close to a student, and something just doesn't feel right. How might you provide feedback to this colleague?
3. One of your colleagues has been asked to mentor a younger faculty member. The younger faculty member often shows up in your classroom in tears, reporting that their mentor is

tough on them. You have coached the young faculty member on ways to have a conversation with their mentor that might help, but nothing seems to be working. How might you provide feedback to the mentor?

4. A colleague in your department has become incredibly negative in your meetings. When not distracted by their phone, the faculty member interrupts others and shuts down ideas. This person's actions have left you dreading meetings that you used to enjoy, and the negativity is having a large impact on your overall satisfaction in your work. How might you provide feedback to your colleague?

5. A student of yours is considering leaving school. You feel that the school is a great fit for this student, and going home would not provide this student the same structure, academic challenge, and opportunities. This student's main reason for wanting to leave is that they feel the coach of their team does not pay attention to anyone other than the "stars of the team." This student wants to play at the next level, and feels that at home they might get more individualized coaching. How might you approach a conversation with the coach?

6. On your residential duty nights, you are struggling to keep the dorm in proper study conditions during the designated study time. As noted in the handbook, students are supposed to be in their own rooms with doors propped open for two hours. Every time you are on duty and asking students to prop their doors, you are told, "You are the only teacher who makes us do this." In your dorm team faculty meetings, the House Head reiterates these rules and gives no indication that the dorm should operate any differently than what the book declares. It is clear from the student pushback that the House Head is not operating consistently with these expectations, which is impacting your ability to do your job as well as your

relationships with the students in your dorm. How might you approach the House Head?

In my opinion, only scenario number 2 meets the standard of reporting to a supervisor; however, every time I conduct this training someone says, "Well, before today, I would have just e-mailed *(name of supervisor)* for all of these scenarios." These poor supervisors! Unless the organization's leaders take the time to build a feedback culture in which adults care to confront one another on their actions and performance, all of this work lands on the shoulders of one or two people. This is ineffective and unsustainable. It is time for adults to take good care of one another, just as they do the young people under their guidance, and begin providing truthful, timely, and trusted feedback to colleagues. Organizational psychologist Adam Grant, in a TED Talks *WorkLife* podcast, recommends that we shift our thinking to view our colleagues as a Challenge Network, a group of people who are going to help you be better at what you do. He also says, "The best way to prove yourself is to show that you are willing to improve yourself."

Like anything having to do with humans and relationships, learning to give and receive honest feedback requires time, patience, and practice. But I guarantee that you will gain trust with anyone you are working with by taking an open approach to feedback, and holding those around you accountable to do the same. And, in so doing, you will experience a healthier environment for your own growth and improvement, as well as the growth and improvement of your students.

CHAPTER 13

Even Better Than One: Teams of Trusted Adults

What is better than one trusted adult? Many trusted adults! Here is the dream and the goal: each young person has multiple trusted adults they can go to, and those adults are all on the same page in supporting that young person. Sometimes I have not been the right trusted adult for a particular student or situation, and I am grateful that I can trust my colleagues wholeheartedly and have the ability to step out of the way and let the good work happen. I have also been in situations when one trusted adult was not enough, and a team approach was needed. Creating and caring for that team of adults, recognizing limits, and evaluating and celebrating efforts based on the goal are the final ingredients in creating a culture that supports adults in building trust and healthy boundaries with young people.

Beyond Small Talk

A former colleague and friend, in his new role as a head of school, regularly sits down with individuals on his team and asks, "Are you thriving, surviving, or drowning?" I love this question. It takes the focus off of the specifics of the work for a moment, to check in with the person. The question implies that this head of school wants this work to be sustainable, fulfilling, and rewarding. He wants his team to thrive. It is in his best interest that each of his team members achieves a sense that they are thriving. First, he needs to know if they feel like they are; if they do not, he needs to know what has to be in place for them to reach that feeling of flourishing.

Too often, when we work together we forget to talk about anything but work. Daniel Coyle writes, in *The Culture Code: The Secrets of Highly Successful Groups,* "Belonging cues are behaviors that create safe connection in groups. They include, among others, proximity, eye contact, energy, mimicry, turn taking, attention, body language, vocal pitch, consistency of emphasis, and whether everyone talks to everyone else in the group." If all it takes is eye contact and turn taking to make someone feel like they belong, isn't that a small ask for a big gain? Trust among colleagues is built in crossover moments and through the seemingly small behaviors that Coyle listed, which remind us we are not one-dimensional workers but full human beings who desire connection with those around us. These connections benefit us personally, and greatly benefit the organization at large.

Because of the vulnerability inherent in working with youth, you might think it would be easier for teachers, coaches, and other trusted adults to really get to know one another. Unfortunately, for many of us, our conversations with the majority of our colleagues don't go beyond weather, food, or updates on the youth in our care. Conversations create connection, this connection can lead us to better understanding, and this understanding can lead us to an atmosphere in which we thrive. The characteristics required for this environment—vulnerability, empathy, conversation, and connection—can get categorized as the "soft stuff." Any time I facilitate an exercise with a group I am working with regularly, I get comments like, "Ugh . . . are you gonna make us sit in a circle and share again?" Pushing back on the sharing of feelings and calling these qualities soft is a way to protect yourself from having to do that work, because in reality, vulnerability and empathy are most definitely the tough stuff.

If you ask questions and actively seek to learn about your colleagues, you will naturally begin to build a more vulnerable and empathetic environment. Here are some options for starting those conversations:

1. Passion
   What fires you up in your work with young people? What do you wake up in the morning thinking about?
   When we wholeheartedly follow our passion, people want to follow us!

2. Relationships
   How do you prefer to interact with your colleagues?
   Asking about dependability, reliability, and predictability will help you get to know your colleague and give you clues for what they expect and prefer in their colleague-to-colleague relationships.

3. Motivation
   What motivates you? What keeps you in your work with youth?
   If passion is what excites us, then motivation is what keeps us moving. You might be surprised by what you learn and how people answer these questions. Here are a few examples I've heard:
   I want to make a difference.
   I just want a paycheck.
   I want to be a championship coach.
   I want to get my master's degree and study x, y, or z.
   I want to be a camp lifer!

These answers will help you to understand your colleagues' motivations, and understanding this will assist you in figuring out the best way to collaborate with this person.

4. Priorities
What are your priorities and what do you understand to be the priorities of our organization?
Time dedicated is how we show and declare our priorities. What we give the most time to naturally becomes what is most important. Your colleagues' choices regarding time will help you understand how their priorities align with yours and how they align with the priorities of your organization.

Actions always speak louder than words, and we really get to know the answers to these questions through observing our colleagues' choices and behavior over the years. I urge you, however, especially when you are new to a team of adults, to move the coffee room conversation away from the weather to deeper topics that will aid in building trust, relationships, and culture.

Savior Syndrome

Over the span of my career I have come to an understanding of my limits and abilities when assisting and advising young people. I have accepted that I can't fix everything and everyone, and cannot hold ultimate responsibility for every problem. I have also run into my fair share of adults suffering from Savior Syndrome, which is how I diagnose an adult who believes they are the only person who can help a child, and that the child, without the care of this particular savior, will suffer. Typically, a person with Savior Syndrome is feeding their own ego with the need to feel needed by the child. This tendency is unhealthy, can blur boundaries, and means that the person is not taking full advantage of the many other skilled adults surrounding a child who can help.

When I was in high school, our school had an honor code that is embedded in my memory to this day: "I will not lie, cheat, or steal, and I will discourage others from such actions." I served on the Honor Council, and students who violated the code would come before the council to state their wrongdoing and await a consequence. It was a successful student-led council advised by two faculty members. One case we reviewed was particularly troublesome, as the young woman before us shared that she had broken the rule because she had chosen not to take her medication, which would normally prevent her from acting in the way she did. I do not remember her infraction, her condition, or the medication, but I remember the conversation distinctly. The council, against my vote, placed the student on citizenship probation.

I had a very hard time with it. I felt as though we were punishing someone for a medical condition, even though we had a note from the student's doctor and psychologist stating that the best thing for her was to accept real consequences for her actions. I still found my seventeen-year-old self, deep within a moral dilemma. So much so that I went on a tirade, questioning the humanity and goodness of the people on the council and our faculty advisors, and then, on the spot, I quit the council and stormed back to my dorm room. Nobody came after me, like I had expected or maybe like I had seen in the movies. I remember getting an e-mail from one of the advisors the next day, the one I had secretly hoped would follow me back to my dorm room, console me, and beg me to rejoin the council. The e-mail very professionally outlined how I could go about formally resigning from the Honor Council.

Looking back, I see that the girl sitting in front of the council was not the only one facing real consequences for her actions that day. I also see that this advisor was not suffering from Savior

Syndrome; she was in it to teach me long-term life skills, and not to soothe my immediate discomfort. Later that day, I received another e-mail. It was from a teacher I respected, who said, "I heard you quit the Honor Council. Want to talk about it?" Immediately, filled with shame and embarrassment for my outburst the night before and knowing that I did not want to actually quit the Honor Council, I said, "Yes, please." This adult helped me craft an apology and ask for my spot back on the Honor Council.

Years later, when I was back working at my high school, the adults decided to let me know that they had orchestrated their response to my outburst that day. They knew I needed to learn a lesson but also that I needed some support. Knowing I had many trusted adults in my corner, the teachers advising the council reached out to another teacher they knew I respected. At seventeen, I wasn't the wiser. At twenty-four, as a brand-new educator, I learned a great personal lesson that I could begin applying in my own work as a trusted adult.

We each play a role in the development of a young person in our care. Sometimes it is offering direct support, sometimes it is drawing the hard line and teaching the tough lesson, sometimes it is being a quiet, available bystander; it is never being the savior. A tag-team approach is key. We cannot do this work effectively if we try to do it alone.

Taking these lessons from my high school years, and from my time as a rookie educator, I found opportunities to apply them daily. As an administrative team in an independent school, at some point in every school year we would say, "Well, we have finally seen it all!" and promptly something more dramatic than the last thing would happen. We dealt with a student who called us pretending to be her own "dying" grandmother so she could get out of a test; students who hotboxed a dumpster; students who broke bones climbing out of windows; and the list goes on. One story that stands out revolves around a young woman who gave me the middle finger behind my back. That was a day to remember.

April was in my acting class, and she was a student I felt I really connected with. On this day, she was upset with me over the way I handled a situation with one of her friends, so, when I turned and walked out of class, she shot me the middle finger. Someone called my name at that very moment, and I turned around just in time to see the gesture. I'll admit, I was hurt. I understood her anger and frustration, but I was shocked it would cause her to act out like this.

As the disciplinarian on campus, I knew it was my job to provide a consequence for this inappropriate action. I also knew that there was much April could learn by working through this breach in trust—and not just that giving the middle finger to a teacher is unacceptable. I also knew that I could not play savior in this situation; my role was compromised.

Just as I had learned from my Honor Council advisors, I found another adult April trusted to help. This colleague advised her in a magical way—without shame or blame—and full of action. This other trusted adult held her accountable and helped us move our relationship to a place better than it had been. I could not thank this colleague enough. The partnership I now have with April lives on, and the work we are able to do to serve the needs of others continues. She is an intern at my camp, volunteers for every event I host, has traveled with me to Morocco, and is making an enormous positive impact on the world. And it is not because of my good work. Without the partnership with another trusted adult, there is no way that April and I would have the positive relationship we enjoy today.

I can't do the work of guiding young people alone, and I don't want to. There have been so many moments of ridiculousness and chaos, moments of tragedy and devastation. So many moments that I did not want to be alone, and would not have survived alone. I need other trusted adults with whom I can share a laugh, bounce an idea, or commiserate. This work would not be nearly as fun, impactful, efficient, or meaningful if done alone. Don't be a savior, don't do it alone, and remember that a team of trusted adults is always far better than one.

Evaluation

The Honor Council advisors in the earlier story were not only advisors to the Honor Council; all had other roles, and they took on advisement as an additional responsibility. One was an English teacher and one was a librarian. It is unlikely that, in their yearly professional evaluation, the feedback addressed their work as Honor Council advisors.

The English teacher was my teacher (if you don't appreciate my writing style, blame her!), and I don't remember a single book or homework assignment from her class. But I know that she changed my life. I find it troublesome that she had probably the greatest impact of any adult on my high school life, yet she was likely never credited for her skillful handling of my council "resignation." Like job descriptions, evaluations can fail to capture the full spectrum of the work; they often focus on the quality of the content or delivery—the "product" we are producing—and not the life-changing service we are providing by taking on responsibility as a trusted adult. Our evaluation systems should be set up to keep the focus where the focus should be: on the young people!

I served on a school task force to create an evaluation system that matched our mission and values. This was no easy task. It seemed as though the common threat of time and resources continued to get in the way of what we all agreed would be best practice. We wanted to evaluate faculty and staff in all areas of their work: academic, extracurricular, clubs, athletics, arts, advising, dorm duty. We were eager to provide 360-degree feedback that would give employees useful advice and ideas in all areas of school life that they touched. To perform this in a way that was both thorough and meaningful, however, would have taken an unrealistic amount of time and energy. Instead, we landed on a rotating schedule. One year you are evaluated in your teaching, the next in your extracurricular leadership, and the next in your Student Life responsibilities (dorm duty/advising/weekend duty). The faculty rotate through the evaluation year by year, receiving feedback in one area of their school life in a continual way.

It was not a perfect system, but it evaluated the employee's participation in school in a more comprehensive way than we had ever done before. Each year, while overseeing all the advisors and providing feedback where necessary, I had the opportunity to focus on fifteen of them in a more thorough way, reviewing their comments, surveying their advisees and the residents of their dorm, surveying the colleagues they work with for Student Life Programming, observing their weekend duty contributions and ideas, and reading their self-reflection, which was specific to this part of their work.

Take a moment to read some of the survey comments from students about their advisors:

- "He is very open and honest. He is good at giving helpful advice. He is very organized and helped me with planning my schedule out during exam week. He is tough on us, well, I guess I would call it tough love. He makes advisory fun, but is serious for serious topics. High school would be much harder for me without him."
- "They are super understanding and accept every person as they are. They are very approachable, and we have a great group but they also treat us all as individuals. They help us a

lot, but not too much, because they want us to be responsible for us. I admire them."

- "She is always honest, sometimes brutally so, and holds all
  of us accountable for our actions and pushes us all to be the
  best versions of ourselves that we can be. She understands
  my constant high school drama and dilemmas. And I trust
  her advice. When she can't meet me in the moment, she
  always schedules to meet me when she can. She always
  advocates for me and helps me out when I need it."

These evaluations and conversations served so many purposes.
I had the chance to share quotes like the ones above with advisors,
whose work is sometimes thankless. These teenagers do not usually
go out of their way to share their thoughts of gratitude with the
adults in their lives. The evaluations gave me an opportunity, as the
supervisor, to sit down with my team one on one and say THANK
YOU! Thank you for your commitment to being a trusted adult
for our students.

The assessment also gave me a chance to filter out any major
concerns with boundary violations and to identify times when an
advisor was not fulfilling their responsibilities. All of this information prompted incredibly important conversations and sent a
strong message to the faculty and staff that this is important work,
and we take it so seriously that we evaluate it. I can't think of a more
important use of time and resources than that. In education, when it
comes to student culture and discipline, we say, "What you permit,
you promote." In our work with adults, I like to say, "What you
evaluate, you elevate." It is this simple. If you are hoping to elevate
your team's services and support for youth, their commitment
to your mission, and their ability to work together—then you'd
better evaluate it.

Celebration

The real celebration in doing the good work with young people does not come for years. And it is hard to wait that long for fuel! Trusted adults invest hours, money, sweat, blood, emotion, and love into young people without any expectation of a return on that investment. Of course, when the struggling player you were coaching hits the home run or the shy student you were working with gets on stage to deliver a speech, you feel good—and those wins should be celebrated. The real fuel in our work, however, comes from the letter that a player, camper, student, or young person writes you five, ten, or even fifteen years later to share that they channel your leadership style through their parenting or in their workplace every day. That one thing you said to them or something they saw you do shaped the way they think, live, and lead. You changed their life, just by being there for them.

Because, unlike in business, there are no numbers to measure this kind of effectiveness and there are no quarterly bonuses to hit, organizations need to get creative about how they celebrate the employees and volunteers doing the hard work of being consistent, caring, and trusted adults in the lives of young people.

I happened to visit a school on the day they were doing their Faculty Farewells. Faculty members who were leaving that school to move to another school, or were changing careers entirely, said their goodbyes to the community onstage and were given flowers while people cried. Whether those teachers were beloved and had worked there for many years, or were leaving under undisclosed circumstances after just one year, they got the same amount of stage time and applause. I turned to a friend who worked there and said, "Wow . . . if this is how you celebrate the people leaving, how do you celebrate the people staying?" She looked at me, confused. "You know, what do you do for the people who have been here serving this school for ten years? Twenty-five years? Who have made this place their life's work?" She responded, "Oh, I think they get a plaque at a luncheon or something. I don't know." It seemed like this school had its priorities backward. Organizations should be publicly celebrating what they want to see more of. I imagine they would like more trusted adults to stay and commit to a long career with them and their young people, rather than leaving after one year.

Something similar happened when I left my last school. There was a large dinner for the faculty and staff, and we each had to choose someone to send us off with a speech. No matter how many years you were there, and no matter how boring, awkward, silent, or scandalous the terms of your departure, a speech was given in your honor. I recognize I sound cynical, but again, celebrate what you want, not what you don't. My colleague, invaluable mentor, and dear friend stood up and delivered a jaw-dropping speech; well, jaw-dropping for me!

> Since the summer of 2010, Brook has brought unbridled positive energy and innovative planning to our school's hidden curriculum. She is a people magnet. Charismatic, spirited, and gregarious, folks of all ages and personalities are drawn to her; she is a veritable Pied Piper. Who among us could ever resist that radiant smile, the sparkle in her eye, and the inescapable invitation to join in—no matter how challenging, wild, or silly the activity is?"

She went on like this for eight minutes! I was overwhelmed. I understand that we want to thank people and show gratitude upon their departure, but I had to leave before I understood my impact, before I felt that my work was really noticed and appreciated. Don't wait until someone leaves or retires to show them their impact, to thank them for their efforts, and to celebrate their presence. I encourage leaders of organizations to think creatively about awards, ceremonies, and what you can do to celebrate trusted adults and never, ever let them underestimate their impact. Following my experience, I am making a strong commitment to let good educators know that I see them, I notice their efforts, and I value their contributions to raising the next generation. We must take the time and make the effort to celebrate one another in small ways more often.

In the news, we consistently hear about the bad adults. The criminals. The ones who are doing it wrong. Those who abuse their power rather than using it for good. Not often enough do we hear about the unbelievable adults who are doing things right. If you have not taken the time lately to thank the trusted adults you had and have in your life, now is the time to do it. Put the book down and pick up the phone. If they have passed, find and tell their family members. I hear the stories, and have heard in the voices of good trusted adults, how much these connections and expressions of gratitude fuel their current and future work with young people. A team of trusted adults needs to create an environment together that aids the work of the one trusted adult, and praises it. At a minimum, we need to show gratitude and celebrate one another. We cannot do this work alone. Get to know your colleagues, invest in your relationships with them, and celebrate one another's commitment to this life-changing work.

Conclusion

There are many situations with adolescents that even a trusted adult cannot prevent. In my time as a teen, there was the night I was babysitting and tried to make Hamburger Helper but somehow managed to screw up—twice—going through three boxes of the mix and three pounds of ground meat by the time dinner was ready. The time I turned red and sweaty when I had to go meet with a banker for the first time by myself. The time I vacuumed up water and coins with a bag vacuum, destroying the dorm vacuum forever. The time I split my pants snow tubing and thought my middle school social life was ruined forever. The time I was hit in the face with a Frisbee. The time I failed a class because I chose not to do the biggest assignment of the semester. The time I offended another student in my class with a culturally insensitive video.

Some discomfort, some embarrassment, and some screw-ups are important ingredients in a healthy upbringing. The point is not to protect or shield young people from the trials and tribulations of life. These character-building moments are necessary, and neither we, nor parents, will always be there to do it all for them. What we can do is do our best to prevent life-altering bad decisions and promote healthy, moral living. And what we fail to prevent, we can respond and react to with compassion and an open door. "Prepare the child for the path, not the path for the child" is a phrase repeated throughout parenting and education books. I believe in it, and also believe in modeling an approach to the path.

I learned the greatest lesson about the approach to the path while on a bike. When I was in college, I took up cycling in the off-season from hockey. I did not look so hot in the full Lycra suit, but I felt powerful zooming around the neighborhood on my newly purchased bike. I met a man out on the road who was experienced and was willing to teach me more about the sport of cycling. In one of our first lessons, he pointed to the path ahead and said, "See that rock?"

"Yup," I responded with confidence, staring right at it.

"Assuming you don't want to hit that rock, what are you going to look at when you're riding toward it?"

"Umm . . . the rock?"

"No, Brook. If you look at the rock, you are going to hit the rock. Eye on the prize. We don't seek to avoid failure, we seek to achieve success. Look directly at the path you want to take, not the path you don't want to take. Got it?"

"Got it."

Staring at the part of the path I wanted to ride, and not the part of it I didn't want to ride, I successfully navigated my way around the rock.

This lesson reaches far beyond cycling, to all areas of life. The path we are aiming for is one of living and modeling an authentic life, striving for health and happiness, taking care of youth, and taking care of each other. If we do our part and model the approach to this positive path, what, then, can be expected of the young people in our care? When I was in high school, my dad said to me, "Whatever you do in life, try your best to end up with friends who are lawyers, doctors, financial planners, car mechanics, travel agents, carpenters, and insurance brokers. If you know someone in each of these fields you should be all set." I have to say, as a grown adult now, this is pretty solid advice. I wish, when I was young, however, someone had also been saying, "It's important you seek out trusted adults." We need to tell young people about the benefits of looking for adults, outside of their parents, they can depend on and learn from. We also need to teach them how to establish relationships with such adults.

Although I was not given specific instruction on how to do this, on one courageous day, I figured it out. As a sophomore in high school, I was sitting in the auditorium when a graduate of fifty years gave a speech after receiving the "Alumnus of the Year" award. I am not sure what breakfast full of bravery I had that morning, but something made me walk up to him after his talk, introduce myself, thank him, tell him how inspired I was by his message, and let him know how much I loved the helicopter alarm clock that he used as a prop during his speech.

The next week I received a package in the mail and upon opening it a helicopter alarm clock kicked on and shot packing peanuts all over the mail room. His hand-scratched note expressed his appreciation to me for reaching out after the speech. My parents had trained me well on the thank-you note front, so I sent him a thank-you note for his thank-you note and included a dancing hamster alarm clock. For years, we went back and forth, thanking each other for each other's thank-you notes. Me, a high schooler, mailing trinkets and notes back and forth with a seventy-year-old man in Chicago. Was he a trusted adult in my life? Not one I relied on daily, but certainly one I knew I could call if I needed. He was an adult figure in my life modeling care and thoughtfulness, and motivating me to do my best in school. He was honored that a young person took interest in his life, his experiences, and his wisdom. I was honored that an older, established man like him would take an interest in my journey and offer me advice for my future.

Whether this man knew it or not, his small, repeated gestures, helped me to keep my eye on the path I wanted to travel. I am forever grateful that I chose, as a fifteen-year-old, to introduce myself to him that day, and to engage with him in the years that followed.

We can only go 50 percent of the way as adults, and the rest is on the young people, who must choose to trust and engage. I want young people to know that there are many reliable adults out there worthy of their trust and ready to support them. We must train young people how to reach out and how to build these relationships. Then, unfortunately, we also need to train them to recognize signs of unhealthy boundaries and potential abuse or grooming. The work of a trusted adult is only as good as the willingness and engagement of a young person. But no matter their position, willingness, or lack of excitement to work with us, we can never give up.

The work is hard, and there is much to read, learn, navigate, and consider. The symptoms of adolescent behavior change, but the need for a trusted adult does not. I choose to keep my eye on the hopeful path, a world where every young person has a safe and healthy relationship with an adult they can truly rely on. If we achieve this, we can combat the risks young people face every day and build communities where everyone has the opportunity to thrive.

You are doing the good work, and young people are watching. Whether you work with young people one day a week, one week a year, or every day, your work matters. Whether you are a teacher or a principal, a camp counselor or a camp director, a volunteer or an organizer, you have the chance to be a leader in this work. You have the opportunity to hold your colleagues accountable, and to keep the focus on teaching the life skills a growing, competent, soon-to-be-adult needs. You, in the singular, are making a difference by modeling a life well lived, and by simply showing up and being present for the young people all around you.

And my final word: I thank you again for the important work you do, I remind you to be the trusted adult you needed when you were young, and I beg you to never underestimate your impact. By building strong connections and healthy boundaries, *one* trusted adult can have an impact on *one* young person that is life-changing, and if *many* trusted adults embrace the privilege and responsibility of committing to be there for *many* young people, well then . . . that's world-changing.

Summary of Tactics for Building Trust, Establishing Boundaries, and Creating Culture

BUILDING TRUST

1. **Declare motive.** I am responsible for your health, happiness, safety, and success. As an adult in your life, this is my job.

2. **Hit the mark.** Set goals *with* young people.

3. **Multiply the self-esteem buckets.** Assist students and athletes in identifying as more than a sport or a stereotype.

4. **Ask questions.** Take the time to ask the questions, and provide the space for students to find their own answers.

5. **Allow for natural consequences.** When possible, allow for the natural consequences (positive and negative) of actions to hold more importance and authority than school- or organization-sanctioned responses.

6. **Be fully present.** Put your phones away and play!

7. **Do something.** Break the mold and do something different— allow your young people to learn something new about you, and give them a chance to teach you something new about them. Busy hands = busy mouths.

8. **Model vulnerability and confidence.** There is connection to be found in learning, trying, and failure. Allow your students to teach you something you have never done before.

9. **Make your messaging consistent and clear.** Work as a team of adults to overtake the negative surround sound with the mission and values of your school or organization.

10. **Model learning to lead and create opportunities to contribute.** Humans need to feel needed. Help to redefine leadership as service, and create opportunities for the young people in your life to feel helpful, worthy, and important.

ESTABLISHING BOUNDARIES

1. **Recognize limitations.** Know your role and know your reporting obligations. One easy way to follow the law and do best by your students is to listen for the words *harassment, bullying, violence, hazing, abuse, neglect,* or *sex*; if these words are mentioned, you should go directly to your supervisor. Do not operate beyond your scope of training or authority.

2. **Base your disciplinary response on organizational policy; do not make it personal.** Understand your organization's policies and commit to upholding them. You have been enlisted to support the rules of your organization, not to write your own. If you want to make change, do so through appropriate channels.

3. **Get what you give.** Your chances of receiving consistency, respect, and fairness from the young people in your care greatly increase when you model these things and expect them of yourself, your colleagues, and your students.

4. **Check your tone.** Pay attention to your body language and tone—they can send as strong a message as your words.

5. **Consciously and cautiously share.** Do not overshare with students. Open up, but always know that what you share with one can or will be shared with all. Choose your words: if you would not say a particular comment at a community meeting, do not say it to a young person.

6. **Use the organization's communication tools.** Stick to the professional tools you have been given to communicate with your students. If texting is a must, discuss logistics only. Texting lends itself to a more casual form of communication, which denotes a more casual relationship and is detrimental to our roles.

7. **Recognize power dynamic.** You are always the adult and they are always the young person. There is a power dynamic— sometimes unseen—at play through grading, playing time, etc. Do not forget that you always hold the power and should be careful not to take advantage of it.

8. **Fill your tank.** Everyone needs fuel to keep going. Be sure your tank is being filled by the success of your students and not their affection. If you need unconditional love, get a puppy! Excessive affection should not be what you need, and is not what students need. More than being told that they are loved, they need to be shown that they are cared for and respected.

9. **Respect the adult relationships they already have established.** Keep your Savior Syndrome in check. The only thing better than one trusted adult is *many* trusted adults. There is room for all to support and care for the young people who are a part of your organization.

10. **Practice self check-ins.** What baggage might you be bringing to the table with each interaction you have with a student or colleague? Check your biases, your ego, and your past experiences, and treat everyone as an individual.

11. **Contain the conflict.** When there is conflict, and there will be, you get to choose to be the gasoline or the fire extinguisher. Ask yourself:

- Is my reaction for me or for the student?
- Am I making this better or worse?
- What is motivating the student right now? What does the student want?
- What is motivating me? What do I want?
- Never be embarrassed to ask for help—ask a colleague or administrator to mediate—you are never in this work alone.

12. **Practice the ultimate shoulder test.** Interact with young people as if their parents are on one shoulder, and your direct supervisor is on your other. How would they react to what you are saying to their child? Then add two security cameras, four phones, and a GoPro filming you—would you want this interaction to go viral?

13. **If you see something, say something.** Take care of your colleagues and hold them accountable. If the actions of a colleague make your eyebrows rise, the hair on the back of your neck stand up, your stomach flip, or it just doesn't feel right—say something.

CREATING CULTURE

1. **Say it, do it, become it.** Talk about who you want to be as an organization, ask yourself if your actions as an organization move you closer to those goals or not. The more you say it, and act toward it, the closer you move to becoming it.

2. **Partner with local organizations.** Reach out to organizations in your area to connect, and help burst the bubble and insular nature of our organizations. Ask what they can do for you and what you can do for them. From advocate organizations to

local law enforcement, experts in this work have funding and enthusiasm for partnering with you to best serve your young people.

3. **Partner with graduates.** If graduates of your program come back to visit and speak highly of their experience, consider it a good sign. If not, there is reason to assess. Consistently ask graduates of your program about their transition to the next level, and what your organization did, or could do, to best prepare them.

4. **Partner with parents.** A strong partnership between parents or guardians and other trusted adults is always what is best for the child. Work to keep communication open and flowing—and keep the focus of that conversation on the needs of the young person.

5. **Cultivate conversations.** We do not need to be experts in understanding every risk our young people are facing, but we do need to be open to having conversations about what is on their mind and what they are seeing in the world: violence, substance use, sex, suicide. Opening the door and creating a space to process events, choices, and actions is the best way to build trust and an open and supportive culture.

6. **Ask for feedback.** Look to your colleagues as a support network of other adults who want to help you be your best. Seek out criticism, have the care to confront, and hold one another accountable for the important work we do for and with young people.

7. **Build relationships beyond small talk.** Building trust with your colleagues is as important as building trust with your young people. Work to shift colleague conversations from the

kids, the weather, and weekend plans to motivation, passions, relationships, and priorities. Knowing each other on a deeper level will build the trust necessary to hold one another accountable and create partnerships that create a stronger culture.

8. **Evaluate what's important.** Assess your organization's evaluation systems. Do they assess the aspects of the job that your organization believes to be most important? Consider evaluating your team as trusted adults rather than keeping the full focus on the primary responsibility listed in the job description.

9. **Celebrate.** Assess your organization's awards and celebration philosophy and practice. Are you celebrating what you want to see more of?

10. **Stay aware of intentional and unintentional impact.** Remember that sometimes we have the greatest impact on another human when we don't even mean to. Pay attention to opportunities for positive impact, even when you aren't intentionally "teaching."

11. **Never underestimate your role.** You are the answer. You are making a difference. The young people in your life will be stronger, smarter, happier, and more successful because of your time, your intentional efforts, and your ability to build trust and model healthy boundaries.

References and Resources

Abelson, Jenn, Bella English, Jonathan Saltzman, and Todd Wallack. "Private Schools, Painful Secrets." *Boston Globe: Spotlight*, May 5, 2016. Accessed January 13, 2019. https://www.bostonglobe.com/metro/2016/05/06/private-schools-painful-secrets/OaRI9PFpRnCTJxCzko5hkN/story.html.

Alphonse, Lylah. "Author Says Praise Is Bad For Kids. Parenting Experts Say He's Wrong." *Yahoo Shine*, January 24, 2013. Accessed November 6, 2018. https://www.popsugar.com/family/Praising-Children-Good-Parenting-26958556.

Anxiety and Depression Association of America. "Children and Teens." Accessed November 21, 2018. https://adaa.org/living-with-anxiety/children.

BBC News. "Catholic Church Child Sexual Abuse Scandal," February 26, 2019. Accessed February 26, 2019. https://www.bbc.com/news/world-44209971.

Bernier, Jetta, Mike Brown, Gregg Dwyer, David Finkelhor, Lisa Friel, Mike Hanas, and Siri Akal Khalsa. "Prevention and Response." *Recommendations for Independent School Leaders from the Independent School Task Force on Educator Sexual Misconduct, 2018.*

Bitsko, Rebecca H., Joseph R. Holbrook, Reem M. Ghandour, Stephen J. Blumberg, Susanna N. Visser, Ruth Perou, and John Walkup. "Epidemiology and Impact of Healthcare Provider Diagnosed Anxiety and Depression among US Children." *Journal of Developmental and Behavioral Pediatrics* 39, no. 5 (June 2018): 395–403. https://journals.lww.com/jrnldbp/Citation/2018/06000/Epidemiology_and_Impact_of_Health_Care.6.aspx.

Bloom, Lisa. "How to Talk to Little Girls." *Huff Post,* June 22, 2011. Accessed June 22, 2011. *https://www.huffpost.com/entry/how -to-talk-to-little-gir_b_882510.*

Brooks, David. "Students Learn from People They Love." *New York Times,* January 17, 2019. Accessed January 17, 2019. *https://www .nytimes.com/2019/01/17/opinion/learning-emotion-education .html.*

Brown, Brené. "Boundaries with Brené Brown." Video Interview. First Aid Arts. https://vimeo.com/274228723.

Century Foundation. "The Benefits of Socioeconomically and Racially Integrated Schools and Classrooms." *The Century Foundation blog,* April 29, 2019. Accessed May 1, 2019. https:// tcf.org/content/facts/the-benefits-of-socioeconomically-and -racially-integrated-schools-and-classrooms/.

Children's Bureau of the U.S. Department of Health and Human Services. "Protecting Children, Strengthening Families." Child Welfare Information Gateway. Accessed October 3, 2018. https://www.childwelfare.gov/.

Coyle, Daniel. *The Culture Code: The Secrets of Highly Successful Groups.* New York: Bantam, 2019.

Damour, Lisa. *Untangled: Guiding Teenage Girls through the Seven Transitions into Adulthood.* New York: Ballantine Books, 2017.

Darkness to Light. "Identifying Child Sexual Abuse." Accessed November 1, 2018. https://www.d2l.org/get-help/identifying -abuse/?gclid=EAIaIQobChMI4tDkqcCs4gIV0MDACh32I w34EAAYASAAEgKFmfD_BwE.

Darkness to Light. "Step 2: Minimize Opportunity." Accessed November 1, 2018. https://www.d2l.org/education/5-steps/step-2/.

Delpit, Lisa. *Other People's Children: Cultural Conflict in the Classroom.* New York: New Press, 2006.

Dobbs, David. "Teenage Brains." *National Geographic,* October 2011. Accessed May 19, 2019. https://www.nationalgeographic.com /magazine/2011/10/beautiful-brains/.

Felch, Jason. "Boy Scouts to Review Half-century of Files on Sexual Predators." *Los Angeles Times,* September 27, 2012. Accessed October 15, 2018. https://www.latimes.com/local/california /la-me-boy-scouts-20120927-story.html.

Felt, L. J., and M. B. Robb. *Technology Addiction: Concern, Controversy, and Finding Balance.* San Francisco: Common Sense Media, 2016. https://www.commonsensemedia.org/sites /default/files/uploads/research/csm_2016_technology _addiction_research_brief_1.pdf

Fiese, Barbara, and Marlene Schwartz. "Reclaiming the Family Table: Mealtimes and Child Health and Wellbeing." *Society for Research in Child Development* 22, no. 4 (2008). https://files .eric.ed.gov/fulltext/ED521697.pdf.

Finkelhor, David. "My Turn: The Path to Preventing Teacher Sexual Abuse." *Concord Monitor,* May 28, 2017. Accessed May 28, 2017. https://www.concordmonitor.com/Preventing-teacher-sexual -abuse-10289136?_cldee=bXNjaGFGFmZXJJAa3VhLm9yZw= =&recipientid=contact-a62760fc38f9e11189240050568300 0d-c6a68971d9874aecb53be7890800870a&esid=e2ad9d0e -7245-e711-8de0-005056bf0011.

Grant, Adam. "How to Love Criticism." *Work Life with Adam Grant* (audio blog), March 2018. Accessed November 6, 2018. https://www.ted.com/talks/worklife_with_adam _grant_dear_billionaire_i_give_you_a_d_minus/transcript ?language=en.

Hardy Girls Healthy Women. "About Us." Accessed January 7, 2019. http://hghw.org/about-us/.

Hess, Frederick M. *Letters to a Young Education Reformer.* Cambridge, MA: Harvard Education Press, 2017.

Hoefle, Vicki. *Duct Tape Parenting: A Less Is More Approach to Raising Respectful, Responsible, and Resilient Kids.* New York: Routledge, 2012.

Jensen, Frances. *The Teenage Brain: A Neuroscientist's Survival Guide to Raising Adolescents and Young Adults*. Toronto: Harper-Collins Canada, 2016.

Lawrence-Lightfoot, Sara. *The Essential Conversation: What Parents and Teachers Can Learn from Each Other*. New York: Random House Pub. Group, 2004.

Maynard, Nathan, and Brad Weinstein. *Hacking School Discipline: 9 Ways to Create a Culture of Empathy and Responsibility Using Restorative Justice*. Highland Heights, OH: Times 10 Publications, 2019.

Meltzer, Ariella, Kristy Muir, and Lyn Craig. "The Role of Trusted Adults in Young People's Social and Economic Lives." *Youth & Society* 50, no. 5 (2018). Accessed May 1, 2019. doi:10.1177/0044118X16637610.

Murphey, David, Tawana Bandy, Hannah Schmitz, and Kristin A. Moore. "Caring Adults: Important for Child Well-Being." (December 2013.) Raw data. *Child Trends*, Research Brief, Bethesda, MD.

National Alliance on Mental Illness (NAMI). "LGBTQ." Accessed October 11, 2018. https://www.nami.org/Find-Support/LGBTQ.

Orenstein, Peggy. "'Girls & Sex' And The Importance of Talking to Young Women About Pleasure." Interview by Terry Gross. Transcript. *Fresh Air*, NPR. March 29, 2016.

Pierce, Cindy. *Sexploitation: Helping Kids Develop Healthy Sexuality in a Porn-Driven World*. New York: Routledge, 2016.

Pittman, Karen J., and Michele Cahill. *Pushing the Boundaries of Education: The Implications of a Youth Development Approach to Education Policies, Structures and Collaborations*. Commissioned Paper #6. Washington, DC: Academy for Educational Development, Center for Youth Development and Policy Research, July 1992.

Plante, Thomas G. "Separating Facts About Clergy Abuse From Fiction." *Psychology Today*, August 23, 2018. Accessed October

15, 2018. https://www.psychologytoday.com/us/blog/do
-the-right-thing/201808/separating-facts-about-clergy-abuse
-fiction.

Scott, Kim Malone. *Radical Candor: Be a Kickass Boss without Losing Your Humanity*. New York: St. Martin's Press, 2017.

Sexuality Information and Education Council of the United States, National Guidelines Task Force. *Guidelines for Comprehensive Sexuality Education: Kindergarten–12th Grade, Third Edition*. Washington, DC: Sexuality Information and Education Council of the United States, 2004. http://sexedu.org.tw/guideline.pdf.

Shakeshaft, C., R. Smith, S. Keener, and E. Shakeshaft. "A Standard of Care for the Prevention of School Employee Sexual Misconduct," *Journal of Child Sexual Abuse*, 2018.

Shallcross, Lynne. "Parents Can Learn How to Prevent Anxiety in Their Children." NPR. September 25, 2015. Accessed February 17, 2019. https://www.npr.org/sections/health-shots/2015/09/25/443444964/parents-can-learn-how-to-prevent-anxiety-in-their-children.

Steinberg, Laurence. *Age of Opportunity: Lessons from the New Science of Adolescence*. Boston: Mariner Books, 2015.

Walsh, Bari. "The Science of Resilience." *Usable Knowledge: Harvard Graduate School of Education blog*, March 3, 2015.

Wilson, Robert R., and Lynn Lyons. *Anxious Kids, Anxious Parents: 7 Ways to Stop the Worry Cycle and Raise Courageous and Independent Children*. Deerfield Beach, FL: Health Communications, 2013.

Wiseman, Rosalind. *Queen Bees and Wannabes: Helping Your Daughter Survive Cliques, Gossip, Boys, and the New Realities of Girl World*. 3rd ed. New York: Harmony Books, 2016.

Youth Development Institute. *Advancing Youth Development Curriculum*. New York: Youth Development Institute, 2014.

Acknowledgments

Thank you to all of the individuals and organizations who provided me with permission to quote substantial information from their research, including Ariella Meltzer, the Youth Development Institute, Thomas Plante, and Darkness to Light.

Thank you to the individuals who were interviewed for the content of this book, with a special thank-you to Kai McGintee, Patricia O'Neill, Perry Cohen, Mary Westover, Susanna Waters, Katherine Keith, Cindy Pierce, and Shanterra McBride.

Thank you to Jill Friedlander for believing in this message, and for helping me write the book I was meant to write. I am so grateful for your expertise, professionalism, and, most importantly, your friendship.

Susan Lauzau, I could not have done this without you! What a privilege and joy it was to work with someone as talented as you. You are the reason this process was as smooth and enjoyable as it was, and for that I am grateful.

Jill Schoenhaut, thank you for being the best project manager in the business. Not only did you pull all of the pieces together in the shortest timeline ever, you had the patience to teach me about every part of the process along the way. Thank you for your ongoing encouraging words, and for all the time you invested in getting physical copies of this book into the hands of those who need it.

To the many friends who tossed around ideas with me, went on endless walks in the woods to discuss, read pieces of the book at midnight, and reworked titles, subtitles, and sentences over and over. Brianne, Caroline, Kristy, Lisa, Eileen, Jody, Kara, Grace, Ashley, Kelly, Anne, Alex, Erin, Deb, Virginia, EJ, KT, Shanterra—I owe you!

Thank you to the many trusted adults who positively impacted my journey at the schools I attended by teaching, coaching, dorm parenting, advising, poking, prodding, encouraging, tough loving, and inspiring me. The Culver Academies, Colgate University, and New York University are very special places full of very special people.

Thank you to my students and colleagues at Kimball Union Academy. KUA is a magical place on top of a hill surrounded by not much more than mountains, swimming holes, and the best deli in all of New England. What fills that school is what makes it extraordinary, and that is the people. The friends I made and the lessons I learned at KUA will be with me for a lifetime. This is a place that puts the work of the trusted adult at the center of all they do.

To the GLC Dream Team and Board Members of Generation Change—a bunch of incredible women committed to making this world a better place for girls and women—thank you! Your belief in my vision, your time, your money, your efforts, and your commitment are something I will never be able to adequately thank you for.

To Cindy and Vicki—when you sat on my porch and told me, "You're next," I could not fathom the journey ahead. Thank you for believing in me, charting the course, and guiding me each step of the way. Cindy—thank you for being a consistent and reliable friend who challenges my thinking, expands my world, and provides a model for all that I aspire to be.

Thank you to my incredible family, and extended families. The Wheeler, Knight, and Raney families are packed full of the craziest, most fun, loving people I know.

My deepest thanks to my husband, Bill, and son, Landen. Thank you, Landen, for giving me the opportunity to be a mother; for testing my theories of adolescence at every turn; for being the wise, loving, and hilarious young man you are; and for being the best adventure partner around. And thank you to Billy, for always supporting and encouraging my dreams. Your belief in me, your wisecracks, your hugs, and your poems keep me going. I love you all the way.

Index

About the Author

Photo © 2019 by Dustin Meltzer.

BROOKLYN RANEY is an experienced teacher, coach, and administrator who has spent the last decade in independent schools. In her free time, she loves to hike, cross-country ski, snowshoe, and travel. Nothing, however, makes her happier than working with youth. She is the founder and director of the Girls' Leadership Camp, a group that hosts a one-week summer camp for middle school girls, as well as one-day boosts and leadership conferences. She is also the founder of Generation Change, a nonprofit that seeks to embolden youth to be empathic and compassionate change makers through cross-generational mentorship.

Brooklyn is a workshop facilitator, speaker, and consultant for schools, camps, and other youth-serving organizations nationally and internationally. She customizes leadership and life skills curricula for schools and organizations, facilitates professional development sessions, and assesses evaluation systems and climate surveys, as well as provides one-on-one coaching for adults on building healthy boundaries.

As a former elite-level athlete at Colgate University and an MA graduate in Educational Theater from NYU, Brooklyn reaches a wide audience with her unique energy, interactive approach, storytelling, and humor. She resides on Lake Winnipesaukee in New Hampshire with her husband, son, and two dogs.

Visit Brooklyn at: *brooklynraney.com*